Praise for *Spiraling*

"Diane Ladd is one of the ا
Her story is unique and dramatic, and what she has learned from
it offers insight to all of us in how to better live our own."
— **Marianne Williamson**, author/lecturer

"From the first word of this volume, I could hear the dynamic,
exciting voice of Diane Ladd. She lives life to the fullest. She lives
to serve, to teach, and to entertain. She confronts life's shattering
challenges, but this has brought profound wisdom, for she has the ear
to hear what her Heavenly Father speaks to her. She has the courage
to confront the medical, political, and professional organizations of
our tumultuous world, but also a penetrating perception to utilize the
best in all these arenas and share it with troubled humanity wherever
she finds them. As she wrote on 9/11 as she walked the streets of
New York: 'I was wrong about that downward spiral; even in great
tragedy, there's an evolution that makes your heart soar. I am
certain of one thing: There are a lot of sides to the word truth.
All of us need to explore all the angles in order to keep our
country free.' Thanks, Diane, for your wisdom and your love."
— **Viola M. Frymann**, DO, FAAO, FCA, director,
Osteopathic Center for Children

"Diane Ladd's book is truly inspiring—a real lesson to
those who have lived, loved, and triumphed over loss."
— **Lainie Kazan**, actress

"Ladd offers some sage advice for anyone interested in
health and in how to live a rewarding life. This book is
both fascinating and educational—a true treasure."
— **Berkley Bedell**, former member of Congress and founder and
chairman of the National Foundation for Alternative Medicine

"In the troubled and complicated field of medicine, it's like a
breath of fresh air to have Diane Ladd bring her compelling
life story to us. In this book, Diane tells us of how she has met
the 'physician within' to overcome pain and illness. The research
she has done and the life she has lived so fully brings hope and
laughter and growth and healing, not just to individuals, but also
to this world, where true healing is so desperately needed."
— **Gladys Taylor McGarey**, M.D.

"A fascinating book. Down-to-earth wisdom and honesty. Will make you understand a woman who has experienced heartbreak and success between tears and laughter. It's wonderful and it's real."
— **Helen Thomas,** Hearst newspapers columnist

"If you're not lucky enough to know Diane Ladd, this book will change that. My bet, you'll want to know her. Her look on life and her perspectives can get you through any day!"
— **Whoopi Goldberg,** actress/comedienne

"I was completely charmed by Diane Ladd's book. It's a deep well of folk wisdom, anecdote, and recollections of a fabulous life. Best of all, it's full of generosity and wisdom. Readers are going to feel as if they've spent a one-of-a-kind evening in conversation with an old friend."
— Best-selling author **Stephen King**

"*Spiraling Through the School of Life* is an extraordinary story of personal transformation. Wise and funny, Diane Ladd weaves a rich and inspirational tapestry of the process of becoming—and being—fully human. This book may change your life and might even help save it."
— **Dean Ornish, M.D.,** founder and president, Preventive Medicine Research Institute; clinical professor of medicine, University of California, San Francisco; best-selling author

"I was deeply touched by this enchanting book. There is much for us all to learn within these pages."
— **Dr. Wayne W. Dyer,** author/lecturer

Spiraling Through the School of Life

Spiraling Through the School of Life

A Mental, Physical, and Spiritual Discovery

DIANE LADD

HAY HOUSE, INC.
Carlsbad, California
London • Sydney • Johannesburg
Vancouver • Hong Kong • Mumbai

Published and distributed in the United States by: Hay House, Inc.: www.
hayhouse.com • *Published and distributed in Australia by:* Hay House Australia
Pty. Ltd.: www.hayhouse.com.au • *Published and distributed in the United
Kingdom by:* Hay House UK, Ltd.: www.hayhouse.co.uk • *Published and
distributed in the Republic of South Africa by:* Hay House SA (Pty), Ltd.:
orders@psdprom.co.za • *Distributed in Canada by:* Raincoast: www.raincoast.
com • *Published in India by:* Hay House Publications (India) Pvt. Ltd.: www.
hayhouseindia.co.in • *Distributed in India by:* Media Star: booksdivision@
mediastar.co.in

Editorial supervision: Jill Kramer
Editorial consultant: Cindy Pearlman • *Design:* Tricia Breidenthal

Library of Congress Cataloging-in-Publication Data

Ladd, Diane.
  Spiraling through the school of life : a mental, physical, and spiritual
discovery / Diane Ladd.
       p. cm.
  ISBN-13: 978-1-4019-0719-8 (hardcover)
  ISBN-10: 1-4019-0719-9 (hardcover)
  ISBN-13: 978-1-4019-0720-4 (tradepaper)
  ISBN-10: 1-4019-0720-2 (tradepaper)
  1. Ladd, Diane. 2. Actors--United States--Biography. 3. Conduct of life.
I. Title.
  PN2287.L135 2006
  791.4302'8092--dc22
                                    2005032218

Hardcover: **ISBN 13: 978-1-4019-0719-8 • ISBN 10:** 1-4019-0719-9
Tradepaper: **ISBN 13: 978-1-4019-0720-4 • ISBN 10:** 1-4019-0720-2

                    09 08 07 06   4 3 2 1
                      1st printing, April 2006

Printed in the United States of America

Dedicated to the children of the world.
Let them stand on our shoulders
in the hopes that they can
see further than we have—
then, maybe, humanity
will really become humane.

CONTENTS

Introduction xiii

PART I: HOW I HELPED MYSELF

Chapter 1:   My Awakening 3
Chapter 2:   The School of Marriage, Divorce,
              Love, and Loss 15
Chapter 3:   My School of Parenting 29

PART II: HOW TO HELP YOURSELF

Chapter 4:   Releasing Anger 39
Chapter 5:   And Now for Some Good
              Old-Fashioned Healing 49
Chapter 6:   Staying Healthy 59
Chapter 7:   Life's Injustices 63
Chapter 8:   Judgment and Forgiveness 71

PART III: MIRACLES

Chapter 9:   An Unlikely Messenger 79
Chapter 10:   Very Special Moments 97
Chapter 11:   The Effect of Helping Others 103
Chapter 12:   My Woo-Woo Story 111

PART IV: FATE, LOVE, AND THE FUTURE

Chapter 13:   Fate 119
Chapter 14:   Love 129
Chapter 15:   Why Men and Women Can Get Along ... 147
Chapter 16:   My Left Foot 155
Chapter 17:   My Mother's Death 161
Chapter 18:   Rising above Despair 167
Chapter 19:   Spiraling into the Future 175

Acknowledgments 181
About the Author 185

INTRODUCTION

O h honey, have I got a tale for you! It's about my great-grandmother Prudence, a woman who delivered more than 3,000 babies in her time before she met her maker at the ripe old age of 95. In the late 1800s, she was known as Aunt Prudie, and she was the only midwife in Pearl River County, Mississippi, population 1,200 hardworking folk, if you didn't count the livestock—which I think some people did in those days.

Whenever a woman's contractions started, my great-granny would "get word," which wasn't a call on her cell phone or via an e-mail. It meant that someone would ride his horse to her front stoop and yell, "I just got word! It's time—a baby's coming."

One winter day in 1926, however, Prudence was the one having the time, and it was a tough one. That big southern sky was dumping snow up to her hip bones when she rode out into the woods to the shanty house of a young pregnant girl whom she feared was having a breech baby—born feetfirst, kicking the world before she could even see it.

The whole darn day was upside down if you asked Prudence, who couldn't see a thing in those woods except sheets of white snow hitting her face and the frozen mane of her horse, who was galloping at top speed.

Suddenly the world slipped out from under her. The horse narrowly missed an old oak tree, bucked, and Prudence was slammed onto the icy, unforgiving ground. The howling winter wind sang in concert with her scream as the big bone in her right leg snapped.

Prudence, who was a goer and a doer, did the only thing possible under the circumstances: First, she cussed, and then she begged the Lord for some forgiveness. She hobbled upright on her good foot, gritted her teeth, and literally climbed back on the horse.

The only howls heard across the county for the next two hours were those of the grateful young woman who delivered a healthy baby girl. After Prudence washed the child, stitched up the woman, and handed over the bundle of joy, she hobbled out of there, rode to the next town, and got her leg set.

I guess you could call that a night's work.

My great-grandmother was 95 years old when she died surrounded by her 33 great-grandchildren, including me. Let me introduce myself . . . back then in Mississippi, I wasn't Diane Ladd, the actress, writer, director, and healer. I was just little Rose Diane Ladnier, a pigtailed girl with a curious nature and this wonderfully crazy Southern family, including my great-grandmother, who was part Cherokee and known in town to have powers that included healing and psychic abilities. I knew her as an incredibly gentle woman with laughing eyes—someone who perfected the art of rolling with life's punches. And, oh baby, she got a lot of fists swung in her direction.

Prudence's husband, Paris, was a teacher, and one day, he just up and told everyone that someday a human would go to the moon on a spaceship and walk around. The townspeople gasped, praised the Lord, and then locked my great-grandfather up in a loony bin. Eventually, they let him go, figuring that maybe he had a point. He was proven correct decades later when Neil Armstrong took "one giant leap for mankind"—including Paris and the rest of the folks in his town.

Meanwhile, they called my great-grandmother "The Mother of South Mississippi" because of all that baby birthing she assisted. When she wasn't delivering the future, she was studying with the Cherokee Indians and absorbing all of their natural and proven healing methods. I tell you, great-grandmother Prudence had all kinds of answers. This was fortunate, because I was a child with all sorts of questions.

As for me, I was born in a little town in Mississippi, population 300. The sign when you entered town read: "Three hundred nice folks and a few old soreheads." (Sadly, in the summer of 2005, savage Hurricane Katrina wiped out that little town, like so many others. My fellow Mississippians have suffered greatly. I can't imagine losing the magical small towns that give this country its soul, and I count myself very lucky to have grown up in one of those special places.)

One day when I was a very young girl, I was lucky enough to be summoned for a little alone time with my great-grandmother Prudence before she went on to heaven. Ohhhh, honey, she had a lot to say to me. I can still hear her rich Southern accent in that comforting drawl that I loved, saying, "Diane, I want to talk to you, child." What followed was like a movie trailer for my own life:

"One day you'll be a teacher, but it will be different from the lady who works at the little school down the road," Great-Granny told me. I didn't understand, but I nodded because I knew that this was one of those times when you just sat there and shut up.

"I also see you in front of a screen, but that will not be your only calling," she continued, leaning in closer as if the really good secrets were about to come out of her mouth. "You'll also command your own audiences. The reason you'll be before a great number of people is that you know things. You'll tell those things to people who need to hear them."

Know things? I wondered. *Know what?* Before I could ask, she silenced me with a look, adding, "Oh, you will also see the world."

Flabbergasted because I had barely been out of my own front yard, I was awed into silence. It might have been the only time in recorded history that this happened.

On that special day, my great-grandmother took this quiet time to unfold her lovely, elderly fingers with skin that looked like a worn road map over her frail bones. She slipped off her treasured wedding ring and put the much-too-big piece of gold into the palm of my hand.

"For luck, honey," she said. "Luck never hurts in this big ol' world."

I felt filled with joy and honored at the same time, but I couldn't express it because someone had a little bit more to say before she went to the Other Side. Great-grandma Prudence was back on that proverbial horse again: "On second thought, you won't need luck," she said, watching me play with the shiny gold band. "You're a lot like me, child."

A lot like her. . . . It took about five decades until I relived her past.

In the spring of 2004, my daughter, Laura Dern, was nine months pregnant and getting ready to have my second grandchild at home. I was all set to be with her, but I had developed a terrible cold a few weeks before the due date.

The doctor prescribed a new drug without telling me one of those usually hidden-in-the-fine-print and serious contraindications. This one was a whopper because the medication could rupture a tendon.

Blinding pain is the only way I can describe the moment when I stepped down and the tendon in my right foot snapped. (I'll tell you the whole story later on.) Weeks later and in a cast from my foot to my knee, I was at home in

California when I got the frantic call that my darlin' treasure was going into labor. Just like my beloved great-grandmother, I was gettin' word.

Unlike Prudence, my horse wasn't parked outside. Luckily, however, I had 300 horses under the hood of my car, so I stood up on my one good foot, gritted my teeth, cussed, and begged the Lord's forgiveness. Great-granny had to navigate the stirrups with her broken leg, and I had to work the gas pedal and the brake with my injury.

An hour later, I sped into Laura's driveway and hopped into her bedroom, where I watched God touch our family as my beautiful granddaughter, Jaya Elise, was born. History had repeated itself, which got me thinking about bigger issues.

I believe that life is a thread, and everything is connected. We're all just somewhere on that thread, hanging on the best we can, as we spiral through our days on this planet. Past to present to future—it's one long spiral. We want to head up, but sometimes we spin down; other times we're just caught in the middle. It's called spiraling through the school of life.

So I'm now known as Diane Ladd, and I'd like you accompany me on a special life journey, which will be grounded in both reality and the metaphysical. It will be about the heart and the head, belief and the unbelievable. It will be serious and seriously funny, but what we really need in this troubled world is to release the tears locked inside each of us. At the same time, we need to find our joy and laughter.

Before we get to the part about how I became a searcher, we have to start with another actress and her belief system. I like to say that before Miss Shirley MacLaine went out on a limb, honey, I was already out on a branch! In fact, at times, I had gone so far out on that branch that I didn't realize that I was standing out there alone on a very thin twig.

But speaking of limbs, I've learned that if you handle a "problem" like a pro, then you won't be left out there on a "limb" by yourself. This book will attempt to help you handle life's problems, so you can either evolve or spiral to your next level.

Why am I an expert? Many people only know me as an actress, director, and writer. Now I'd like you to meet the other Diane Ladd: I'm a Southern woman guided by my intuition in both my show-business and health-healing work. I was born with a certain amount of psychic ability, and I'm what they call a "high intuitive." I'm also an ordained minister. So basically, I can entertain you; if that makes you sick, I can heal you. And if that doesn't work . . . honey, I can bury you! Let's just say that I'm a very good friend to have around.

However, you'd think I was the stupidest blonde you'd ever met if you saw me trying to figure out my new Treo 650—my phone, camera, address, e-mail, and Internet system all in one. It does everything but wash the dishes and I can't work the thing. My gifts lie elsewhere, you see.

For instance, I'm a member of the board of advisors for the National Foundation of Alternative Medicine (NFAM) in Washington D.C. I've devoted decades to working as a nutritional lecturer, consultant, medical intuitive, and healer in association with many notable American Medical Association doctors.

Perhaps my biggest qualification for writing this book is my true desire to share some of my amazing experiences and the information I've learned from a rewarding and sometimes-difficult life. I hope that these pages may bring comfort and inspiration to others. Perhaps you'll even see yourself in my words.

Life forced me to learn many lessons, and now I want

to share what I've discovered by listening with my heart—it has very big ears. Let this country girl explain: The American Indians say, "Before you judge a person, you must walk in his moccasins." How far? Twenty miles—and if *you* can walk that far in moccasins, good for you, baby.

I've spent decades doing research on the topics you'll read in this book. But more important, I went through it all—including marriage, divorce, and the loss of a child—by simply living a life that defied even my own expectations.

In my studies, I've learned that science uses the spiral as a symbol of all energy. I believe that we're all circling the tree of life as we evolve. What goes up has got to come down; what comes down needs to go back up. The latter is the real tricky part.

We spin down, around, and up. You can also keep spiraling down, but that's ultimately up to you. When you're evolving as a person, you're moving up. Sometimes when you're too involved and consumed by the drama of everything around you, it's hard to evolve. And doesn't that happen to all of us?

Every person has the possibility to go up as high as he or she wants to go, but you have to be able to kick dirt and work really hard to do it. You can't just expect your upward spiral to come naturally. It's a careful step-by-step learning process. If you don't deal with one part of your life or one of your steps, you won't evolve in other ways and make it to the next level.

Think of it like this: You can't put food on the table unless somebody grows it, picks it, and delivers it to you. Then you wash, cook, and serve it. That's a lot of steps for a meal.

So what makes people think life should be so easy? It's also a series of actions, and often it's not easy. But what I've learned is that life isn't as difficult as people make it . . . you just need to follow some simple lessons that I'll share with you in this book.

We'll start at the beginning: I'll explain in the first part how I helped myself, and then reveal how you can help yourself in the second section. I hope to defy some of your preconceived notions and expectations with the third and fourth parts—"Miracles" and "Love, Fate, and the Future."

Since I'm a Southern gal, I'll offer you vignettes from my own life in a loose, laid-back way. Imagine that we're sitting on the front porch together and sharing the secrets of the world over a tall glass of sweet tea on a lovely summer afternoon. This Introduction has already given you a taste of what to expect—you'll meet many more folks who are as fascinating as my great-granny Prudence.

🌀

If I can help one person in this world, then I've done my job, and it's enough. Even if you help yourself, that's enough.

I marvel at the miracles around me, and I wrote this book for a simple reason: People are desperate for any bits of wisdom, and I hope to give you what I've learned during my time on this planet. These days we live in a world that's full of conflict, where some folks are so corrupt that hell wouldn't even have them. But the good news is that I think the world is poised for change.

We're in the cycle before the revolution. As we get ready, it might help to use a little Southern wisdom that my great-grandmother Prudence might enjoy. This is my motto (repeat it out loud): *Have a little faith, kick a little dirt.*

🌀 🌀 🌀

PART I

How I Helped myself

CHAPTER 1

MY AWAKENING

All my life I'd been waiting for my "profound experience" to happen, and I figured that there might even be a helping of thunder and lightning on the side to let me know that this was my Big Moment. How Hollywood of me! I was waiting for a brilliant cloud to manifest itself, and with it bring the revelation of the ages . . . but it didn't happen like that at all for me.

Instead, in 1982, I made my pilgrimage home to the farm in Mississippi to see my ill father. My mother and dad came from two entirely different backgrounds—she, from an aristocratic, genteel Alabama world; and he, from a wild Tennessee Williams Mississippi-country lifestyle. Daddy spent his entire life helping chickens, cows, horses, goats, pigs, and dogs heal. He was a veterinarian who saved thousands of animals and helped poor farmers with their livestock. But there was no helping Daddy heal that summer, and following his death, I went to a nearby beach to ask God for answers.

One sunny morning, I took a long, solitary run that had me splashing through the shallow water of a beautiful, small cove. Slowing to catch my breath, I sat down in the sand to contemplate the sky. The enormity of the vast blue expanse that was my universe made me feel as if I were swirling inside myself.

Suddenly, a heady sense of life seemed to envelop me. As if to escape a moment this powerful, I turned sideways. My eye caught a spiral shell, the most perfectly formed mollusk I'd ever seen in my life, a nautilus.

Holding it in the palm of my hand, I considered the magnificence of the spiral, including its shape, form, substance, and relativity to all life as we know it. My profound moment was the thought that each of us human beings spiral through life with all of our needs, lessons, and emotions moving upward or downward at any given moment—but not staying static.

We humans travel up and down the spiral again and again throughout our lives. It makes sense that even in our lowest moments, such as my state after my beloved daddy eventually passed away, a spiral upward again is just a breath away.

My pattern began when I was a little girl. I don't know why, but every night of my childhood, I said goodnight to Mommy and Daddy and then prayed for wisdom. I wish I could tell you that this was for a particularly lofty reason, but mostly I just thought it sounded good. Wisdom—I want some of that stuff! It even sounded delicious, although it might have been better at that age with some praline ice cream and chocolate sauce thrown on top of it. (Heck, those fixins' would still make *anything* better at this age!)

When I wasn't searching, I was just living the life of a little girl in the Deep South, a place that gave this child room to think. I didn't see giant buildings when I stared out my bedroom window. Instead, my eyes were filled with sky, sun, and stars. It was a wonderful emotional canvas.

My daddy was a good, kind man who always told me, "Diane, you can do anything you want. Just put your mind to it." My mother was a very sweet, graceful, gracious lady who only had one child—me. But I had tons of cousins in Mississippi, because the rest of my relatives were very prolific when it came to reproducing themselves.

My little family was different because I didn't have any siblings. I didn't know it at the time, but only children like myself try to adopt the whole world. We want to share our words and experiences because we're so glad to have somebody there to listen. If another kid came over, he or she could have all of my toys and candy because I was so glad to communicate with another human being . . . and that feeling has never left me.

As I told you earlier, my great-grandmother Prudence was a doctor and healer who studied with the Cherokee Indians. In addition, several of my aunts were highly intuitive and psychic. "Child," said my great-granny, "I know that there's some of that in your blood, too."

I kept that news quiet at my Catholic school (one of the few in the area), where my class consisted of seven children, and the high school population topped out at 35 kids. There were very few Catholics and Jews who also attended the Catholic school in our town, but my first boyfriend was Louis Rosenbaum. My mother thought he was very handsome with his beautiful teeth. Daddy's people were all hard-shelled Baptists.

There were three girls and four boys in my class, and we certainly made the most of all that attention from our teachers. One girl became the first to lead a car company in the state of Mississippi, and another girl went on to be the head of a university. I became an actress, writer, and director. One of the boys went off to be a priest, changed his mind, and ended up as a writer. The other three boys became millionaires.

Those nuns did something for us, didn't they? They were strict teachers, and they gave their lives to us. We didn't get away with anything. They taught us perseverance and the idea that we had to work hard in this world. They also showed us the merits of living with integrity and speaking the truth, and most important, caring about our fellow human beings. These were great life lessons.

I was a very inquisitive child, but also a good girl. I remember one day when I went to church with my boyfriend to pray during our lunch hour. Well, here came the nun, who treated this as if we were committing a major sin that included bodily fluids! I was embarrassed for her because we weren't swapping spit—we were swapping prayers. I learned that it takes all kinds, including all types of nuns, to make a world. On that day, however, I didn't say a word because I was a little bit afraid of that particular teacher.

My astrological sign, Sagittarius, provides its beneficiaries the opportunity to be spiritual seekers, and even as a child, I was different. The other girls and I would be playing this wonderful jump-rope game called "Mayonnaise." We'd jump while calling out the letters: M-A-Y-O. . . . I never got past the O. Mostly, I didn't jump at all during recess or lunch.

Instead, I'd go to church and pray during my lunch hour, and I often had other children—out of curiosity—follow me into the sanctuary. One time when I was ten years old, a nun even came in and asked, "Who are the kids who went to pray at lunchtime?"

All my classmates pointed at me, because they thought they were in trouble.

"Diane, you helped save a man's life," the nun told me.

That day I'd seen a man sitting in our church looking despondent. His wife and child had been killed in a terrible car accident, and he wasn't sure how he'd go on. He was completely heartsick.

On this particular day, he'd bought some nasty old pills and was on his way home to end his life. He was in his car, crying about the idea of killing himself, when he passed our school. He knew that it was lunchtime, and he saw a group of children going into church with no nun ordering them to. He realized that we were giving up our lunch to pray. The man said that in the minute he saw us enter the building on our own accord, he decided that he wanted to live.

As the nun told me the story, I thought, *Whoooeee, I saved a life! Oh yeah—that's good! I'm gonna be a saint!* So I ran over to the church later that day and sat looking at all the pictures of the saints. Forgive me, God, but I stole all of the holy pictures lying around in church and put them in my bedroom drawer.

The next day, I asked the kids to come pray with me, but they refused. "You go ahead and play your silly lunch games. I'm going to be a saint," I told them. I opened the church door all by myself and suddenly heard angelic music coming from inside. I'm sure that it was just Bishop Tulane's choir practicing for Sunday. But on that day, it didn't seem like an earthly rehearsal—it sounded like angels who might be there to take a little girl up to heaven.

In the blink of an eye, I slammed that big ol' church door shut and went to play Mayonnaise with everybody else. Sainthood could wait! That halo I imagined around myself was actually a cowardly yellow streak up my back as I ran to join the chanting girls: "M-A-Y-O . . ."

When I was very young, like all children, I had dreams of what I was going to do when I grew up. I wanted to be a district attorney and solve hidden problems or maybe even be a leper-colony missionary and save people. I also had some highly intuitive experiences. Once when we went to church while visiting my aunt in Alabama, the little altar boy was flirting with me, but I was mostly ignoring him. All of a sudden, there was a flash of light before my eyes.

For no reason at all, I began to silently pray: "God, if you let me be an actress, I'll help build you a church someday." Then the moment was over, and I went back to flirting with the altar boy. I don't know why that actress comment came from inside of me, except that perhaps I was one in a former life. "You're a drama queen, all right," Daddy used to tell me.

At age 15, while still in Mississippi, I did a few plays. Then one night when my family was in New Orleans, I asked the great Pete Fountain to let me sing a song with his band. And he did! In fact, he told my father, "This child is a singer. You've got to encourage your daughter." Daddy thought he was nuts.

I graduated from high school at the age of 16 and went to New Orleans to do a play, despite the fact that I had a scholarship to study law. My parents allowed me to do the show as long as I attended a very fancy New Orleans finishing school.

This was at a time when big bosoms were all the rage. So at the finishing school, they instructed the girls to wear bras that had plastic pads inside them; you were given a straw to "blow up" your bosoms several times a day to have the perfect figure. Unfortunately, they forgot to tell one poor girl not to get on a plane with that contraption. Her bust blew up at 25,000 feet! I thought that all that energy focused on vanity was a pitiful way to waste time, especially when I was busy following my destiny.

When I was 17, I moved to New York City, but then I got word that my father was very sick in Mississippi. To make matters worse, his business partner left town with all of Daddy's money while he was on his sick bed. Thankfully, Daddy recovered, but financially he was down and out.

You always hear about prejudice in the South, but the black people in our town always loved my father. After his recovery, I remember him telling me a story when I was home visiting that made his chin quiver. He said, "Diane, when I got better, I didn't have a cent. And it's funny how when you don't have any money, some of your friends just disappear off the face of the earth.

"I took my clothes over to the cleaners the other day, and when I went to pick them up, I tried to pay the owner [who was black]," Daddy said. "The man told me, 'Oh no, Mr. Ladnier. I'm not taking your money, sir.'"

"Why not?" Daddy asked.

"Well, as kind as you've been to me and mine, you think I would take your money when you've been down and out and sick?" the man replied.

Daddy started to cry while telling me the story, and tears rolled down my face when he said, "Diane, that man is my only true friend, and he's a black man." That was a major lesson in life for my Daddy and me.

After making sure that my father was really feeling better, I went back to New York, where I had auditioned as a dancer for the famous Copacabana. It was for a three-month stint; afterward, they'd hire all new performers. More than 500 girls auditioned with me, and the Copa chose 12, plus one captain as a swing girl. (This meant that she knew each girl's position and filled in on other dancers' nights off.) I was one of the chosen—yeah!

On Saturday nights, I'd do the show, shimmy out of my sparkling costume, and then march myself right to church for the late-night Saturday mass. The service was specifically for show people who wanted to cleanse their souls.

One night I sat next to a very poor woman whose purse was open, so I could see that there was almost nothing in it. Quietly, I took the $25 I'd earned that night and put it in her purse. A few days later, I got two modeling jobs! This was my proof that if you do good, then good will come back to you. I still hold that belief today.

I stayed in New York and got other dance jobs and worked as a model before finally landing small roles on TV. Once, when I didn't have any money, I passed out fruitcake at Bloomingdale's. I'll never forget one day around Christmas when this society matron stopped eating her cake to ask me, "Wait a minute—didn't I just see you starring on the TV show *Naked City?*"

"Yes ma'am," I answered. "Have another piece of cake."

I lived in a $75-a-month walk-up apartment, a one-room place that was my home. I was never afraid, because the Universe was protecting me. Life was very hard back then, but I studied like mad with a fantastic actor named Harry Guardino. He made his students do an acting exercise where he told us that we were walking into a shack, and then we were instructed to look around and imagine what was inside. Afterward, Harry criticized me.

"Diane, you went into that imaginary shack, but you didn't really look around. How many cobwebs were there? How many loose boards?" Harry demanded.

"What are you talking about? I've been in shacks with my daddy! Don't you tell me what to look for in a shack!" I ranted.

"Why do you think you're such a great actress, Diane?" he suddenly asked sarcastically.

"Because I was conceived to be a *great* actress—and given birth to become a better one," I said.

And Harry just let it go without another word.

When I was young, I got to watch some of the movie greats do their work—icons such as Bette Davis, Barbara Stanwyck, and Spencer Tracy. I also observed stage actors, including Kim Stanley, Helen Hayes, Ralph Bellamy, and Jason Robards. I was even lucky enough to have the opportunity to work with some of them and observe their professionalism and skills.

You need to be around the best in order to learn. These actors' brilliance expanded my gifts and creativity. They carried me out of my own body. Just watching them, I felt as if I were a part of their glory.

I also learned in those days that the truly great human beings were the most gracious. I'm not saying that they didn't have tempers or say caustic things once in a while, but most of the time they were just plain wonderful and loving to all people. It's the amateurs in life who are the most egotistical and want to play the "power monger." I'm not just talking about show business—this applies to any realm of life including personal relationships.

Back in those days, I wasn't into issues of healing—I was a rascal who was just living her life. But for my acting work, I decided to take a course on modern dynamics from Dr. Jules Bernhardt. He was one of the first to teach that the mind is powerful enough to heal the body.

I was in a class one day doing an exercise where you had to pull in light through your head, send it through your heart, and then move it through your hands to heal. Walking around to help the students, Dr. Jules stopped in front of me and gasped.

"Good God!" he exclaimed. "Diane, you're a healer. Let me feel your hands."

This was the first time I realized that I had this gift. It might sound strange, but I'd never noticed this as a child or a teen-ager. That moment in class was an epiphany for me, although I'd later find out that many actors have healing energy in them. They use it nightly onstage and often send it out across the footlights. Yet I was surprised to notice the powers within myself.

I'd also come to know that in order to be a great healer, you need to practice and work at it. Now I can recognize when the urge to heal builds up within me. I know that I need to help someone, and I simply can't turn that feeling off. When I was much younger, I wasn't sure what that sensation meant because I hadn't practiced using my talents.

After that class, word got around, and if someone had a headache, they'd come to me to take it away. I'd never done that before in my life (at least to my knowledge). In the meantime, I was down to my last dollar, hungry, and broke—but God always brought me a job. At one audition, the casting people even offered me a beer! I figured it was food and drank it, and I was tipsy all day.

I'll never forget auditioning for *Orpheus Descending*, written by my cousin Tom Lanier Williams, aka Tennessee Williams. I was so nervous at my audition, and I hadn't eaten well that morning. I went to the bathroom and even vomited before my turn came, but I got the role.

The playwright wanted the play to be a hit so badly, but it just wasn't working. "That ending is not good," I told my cousin (whom I called Tom—ah, the bravado of the young!).

"Why don't you rewrite it?" Tom said . . . so I did.

I performed in my first off-Broadway play, *and* I got to rewrite Tennessee Williams! Talk about an upward spiral.

During the times when I wasn't auditioning for other shows, I'd go to the Salvation Army and buy boxes of books from dead people's estates. For $2.50, I could get a whole box, and when I was through reading, I could bring some back and trade them in!

As I mentioned, at the age of 16 I turned down a scholarship to Louisiana State University to study law. Instead, I embarked on this show-business path, but it's not as though I left learning behind. By the time I was 17, I realized that I wanted to continue my education, and the Salvation Army books were my guides.

The volumes I bought all seemed to be connected by a common thread weaving through religion and metaphysics. I studied mind dynamics, karma, Indian traditions, and the Kabbalah during a time when nobody dared to even admit that these topics existed.

By the time I turned 18, I realized that this wasn't my only life . . . I knew that I was here in another time and place. I began to ask: *Why are we here? What are we doing? What's this play called life really about? What's our mission, our goal?*

My curiosity sparked, I began a four-decade search for the truth about life. But before I get to my observations, let me tell you about the experiences that formed them.

CHAPTER 2

THE SCHOOL OF MARRIAGE, DIVORCE, LOVE, AND LOSS

What can I say about my ex-husband Bruce Dern? I can only tell you that he's one of the most incredibly brilliant actors to ever come out of this country. The man is in a class with actors such as Jimmy Dean, Montgomery Clift, and "The King," Marlon Brando, who was my friend.

Bruce and I costarred with the greats, including Jack Nicholson, Robert Duvall, and Robert DeNiro. We also did three films together: *Rebel Rousers;* an avant-garde film called *The Wild Angels,* which won several awards; and later, *Mrs. Munck,* which I wrote and directed.

Brando's *The Wild One* had been censored in England a decade earlier. But when *The Wild Angels* was released there a decade later, people were lining up to see it, resulting in an unexpected bonus: Hollywood finally was allowed to release the earlier, controversial picture, *The Wild One,* in the UK.

Bruce and I did two plays, *Orpheus Descending* and *Only the Good Die Young.* We met during *Orpheus.* I was portraying Carol Cutrere (an idealist) opposite another actor who played the male lead of Val Xavier, or Orpheus. That man suddenly got a great part in a big Broadway production, and the person chosen to replace him was a new hotshot named Bruce Dern.

He'd just appeared in small roles in two Broadway shows and was starring in the successful Elia Kazan film *Wild River,* for which he had garnered terrific reviews alongside the great Montgomery Clift. He was newly divorced, smart, creative, and on fire—in a word, he was irresistible. I guess you could say Orpheus had descended!

Bruce and I fell in love when we were very young, connecting through the creativity in both of us. The arc of emotion was forged by mutual respect, with an intensity we couldn't deny. We both felt as if we'd come home. We were young and in love, but we were also poor, since the off-Broadway salary was only $65 a week in those days. When tragedy later hit our lives and tore us asunder, we were too poor to be able to pull the shades down and keep the ugliness out.

Struggle defined us, but nobody could keep me laughing through my tears like the man who'd become my husband. The problem was that there'd be too much crying. We couldn't have known that we were about to face the darkest times of our lives.

What was good and rich and right between us manifested itself through a miraculous merging of our DNA when I became pregnant. It seemed like a miracle, because after numerous tests during Bruce's first marriage, medical doctors had informed him that he was sterile. We discovered that they were wrong.

A lot of people seem stranded in life, but Bruce was one of the loneliest men I'd ever known. An inner searching and desolation had been present since his childhood and maybe beyond. My heart went out to him—and it was easy to give him my heart because he was so handsome.

Love is a word that I take seriously, and I realize that there are all kinds of caring. Even today, I'm still amazed by the profound depth of that very word, and after all these years,

I'm still learning. Bruce had his own definitions of love. He came from a very wealthy family, but they were also cold and distant. The sad truth is that for all their money and supposed elegance, I don't think they understood the richness of true affection. Perhaps it was Bruce's karma to overcome this in his lifetime.

My family of origin may have struggled with their own inadequacies, but I experienced warmth and connectedness as a child. There was always time for a hug.

I'm sure that most people hope that their first marriages will be the only such union in a lifetime, but it doesn't always work out that way. A lack of maturity, self-awareness, and wisdom forms our thoughts and actions. For example, I remember this one time when I made a beautiful meal for Bruce from scratch and waited for him to come home so that I could light the candles.

He walked into the kitchen, took one look at the gorgeous meal and the flickering light, and exclaimed, "Damn! I can't even see the food!" He didn't really mean anything by it—after all, men and woman are so different. Still, my feelings were hurt, and instead of crying (which is what I wanted to do), I lashed out and yelled harsh words not easily taken back.

Anger became a tangible current between us . . . it was a reliable and known commodity. Back in those days, there was nobody to tell us what you do in a marriage. We didn't rely on therapists or Dr. Phil on TV—we were just coping the best we could. We were two actors who were bravely facing the world, looking for work, and worried that we'd be homeless the next month because we couldn't pay the rent. We didn't know how much life would extract from us emotionally in the coming years.

Love and Loss

Before the pain entered my marriage, however, there was the joy. Bruce and I became the parents of a treasured daughter named Diane Elizabeth Dern. Then in 1962, my beautiful 18-month old baby girl died when she fell into our swimming pool. When she tumbled into the water, she hit her tiny head, causing a massive brain hemorrhage. She couldn't be revived.

As the days passed following our baby's death, Bruce and I were consumed—hearts, minds, and souls—in a river of loss. We felt so hopelessly adrift in the emotional pain of our own private hell that I didn't think we would ever recover. It was as if God had cracked me open like a walnut to get at the sweet meat of my soul . . . but I felt soulless. My world became black and white: It was just pain and merciful sleep, sleep, and unrelenting pain.

There were times when I honestly believed that I was being dragged by my shoulders through the underworld in order to get to heaven someday. I wondered if there would be any pieces of me left for salvation; I was like Humpty Dumpty in that there wasn't much that could be put back together again. It was the lowest spiral of all.

However, there were kind acts for which I'm still grateful. The day of my child's funeral, friends came to our home, but I was locked in my bedroom. At one point, I finally decided to go into the living room to greet them.

I saw my friend Jane Anne Dow, who'd been thrown off a horse and broken her back and neck. She heard the doctors in the hospital say, "Well, she'll never walk again."

"I *will* walk again," she vowed, and by the day she came to our home, she was on her own two feet, but with her neck in a brace. She walked around my living room, graciously serving sandwiches to the guests. A woman dropped a drink, and Jane Anne painfully bent to pick it up. The woman said, "Let the maid pick it up."

But we didn't have a maid; what we *did* have was a friend who was in a brace but would do anything to help us. I'll never forget standing there in my bedroom doorway and looking at this lovely soul who'd been given hopeless news, yet here she was, proving the doctors wrong and serving everyone else. She was a lifeline of hope and possibility, and that registered deep in the recesses of my heart.

As the days passed, my body went into shock and I started to develop fevers and strep throat. My physical self was also screaming at me to replace my lost child, but the doctors gave me little hope.

There was just so much hurt inside that I didn't know how I would make it through the day. I sobbed into my pillow, trying to release the pain while praying that God would grant us a second chance at parenthood. Amazingly, six weeks after my daughter's death, I became pregnant again. I remember laughing with such joy through my anguished tears. God taketh away and He giveth back! At least that's how my mind reasoned what was happening to us—but it wasn't that simple.

Within that altered state of grief, loss, and renewed hope (and a few weeks pregnant), I began rehearsals for a play called *The Wall.* I'd won the coveted role of a Jewish heroine named Rachel Apt. It was a beautifully written, true story about the Jewish ghetto and the horror that Nazi Germany and Hitler had perpetrated. I thought that I could use my life force and talent to tell the story of so many who lost so much; I wanted to give a voice to so many children who never should have died.

One afternoon on my way home from rehearsals, I began to feel ill. I could tell that something was wrong, and I began to panic. I drove to the nearest doctor's office and told him with great emotion that I was scared to death because I was pregnant. "Something is very wrong!" I cried.

The doctor kept staring down at my left hand, which made me realize that because of the play I wasn't wearing my wedding ring. Suddenly, I knew what he was thinking. He decided that I was just a single, pregnant girl who must be seeking an abortion. The man refused to examine me and actually pushed me out of his office.

In extreme physical pain, as if my insides were on fire, I searched for the nearest hospital and made my way into their emergency room. A grave-faced doctor gave me horrifying news: "We think you might be experiencing a tubular pregnancy." Then he did a test, which included inserting a needle through my stomach into my womb and withdrawing blood. If the blood clotted, that meant that it wasn't a tubular pregnancy.

It clotted! The doctor soothed and calmed me. Eventually, the pain began to disappear, but the cause of it was still unknown.

A little over a month later, just before a performance of the play, I began to feel very ill again. I experienced a tapping on the back of my neck and had blurred vision, fever, and severe abdominal pain. The theater called an ambulance, I was rushed to the hospital, and it turned out that I was hemorrhaging. Sadly, the original test had been wrong, and I did have a tubular pregnancy—which could have cost me my life because the tube was bursting. I was rushed into surgery immediately.

They removed my right fallopian tube and five-eighths of the left one: Peritonitis had set in from the tubular pregnancy, and I was about to die. The inclination in this type of case back in those days was to perform a complete hysterectomy. Luckily, I had a brilliant and prudent surgeon who left quite a bit behind. He wanted me to have enough female organs so that I could function as a woman and have my period, so he left both ovaries and three-eighths of one tube.

"I'm sorry, Diane," he gently told me. "It's absolutely impossible for you to have another baby."

Over the next year, I consulted with five renowned gynecologists. One after another told me, "I'm sorry, but it's impossible. You'll never have another child."

My reply was always the same: "I *will* have another baby," I answered with quiet determination. The doctors thought I was nuts.

I am my father's daughter. During this time, I remembered how our next-door neighbor's son in Mississippi contracted spinal meningitis. The Mobile, Alabama, hospitals were filled to the brim with similar cases, so the doctors told our neighbors to take their son home because he'd be dead by morning. Those poor parents were informed that nothing could be done to save him.

I remember my daddy standing in our doorway, the boy's father tearfully pleading with him to save his son's life. Daddy kept telling him that he was a doctor for chickens and livestock, not people. As his eyes filled with empathetic tears, my father also told the desperate man, "You don't ever give up on life as long as you're *in* life."

Then Daddy went out and found a country doctor. As fate would have it, this young man had just graduated from one of the most prestigious medical schools in the country, and my father rushed him to our neighbor's house. The doctor worked on that boy all night. You could hear the boy's screams all through the neighborhood, but the child lived.

Remembering that event, I decided that I would find my own miracle. In 1963, there were no health stores, and I could only find one somewhat-relevant book on the market. It was Gaylord Hauser's *Mirror, Mirror on the Wall.* I read and reread the book from cover to cover but couldn't find any doctors involved in alternative modalities. Vitamins and minerals were subject matters that were rarely discussed, so I spent my days in libraries searching for answers or even a tidbit of information.

Weary and increasingly disheartened, I took a trip to see a specialist named Dr. S. Peller, an amazing human being who'd served in the British army with Lawrence of Arabia. Born in Vienna and kicked out of his country because he wrote a book on abortion, he still became a famed heart specialist. He was the type of man who'd never leave his patient's side, and he was another giving angel who entered my life.

I told him about my dream of having another child with what was left inside of me. Then I braced myself, waiting for him to tell me the awful truth that there was no chance. Dr. Peller looked at me and quietly said, "Who said you couldn't have another child? You don't have to give up. You don't know what God has in store. I've seen many miracles in life."

He told me to explore vitamins and investigate regular mud baths. "Mud baths!" I whooped. "I guess I should have just stayed in Mississippi!"

"Why, you might want to go down there for a while, relax, and soak in some good old American mud," he said. "Mud baths prevent sterility. It's all about the earth."

I didn't make it all the way back to my childhood home, but instead went to Palm Springs and sat in all the mud I could find. In more than one of the well-known resorts that define the area, the stuff is sterilized. I still couldn't help but sit there, sinking into that dirt, thinking, *Did the heat they used really kill all the "things" in here?*

It was squishy, icky, gooey mud all the way up to my neck. I wish I could say that I had an epiphany by becoming one with the earth, but it wasn't that way. It was just gross, but I did it—I would have sat on hot coals if they told me it would help me have a baby. I did days of these mud baths and thought about how the goop really is healing, since the minerals it contains, including magnesium, are what we're made of as human beings. It makes more sense than ever when we hear the saying, "And to the dust they shall return." In the meantime, the good dust might help you bounce back—and fast!

Certain Indians teach that in some cases, when someone is injured or dying, covering their body in this organic substance can save them. The Cherokee tribes depended on mud as a healing device. They'd put leaves and herbs over a wound—with mud on top of that—to draw out impurities, heal the problem, and cleanse the body. Perhaps we've forgotten more than we'll ever learn in this lifetime; sometimes the old ways are the best.

For two years, I did the mud baths and worked on my body inside and out. Then, as part of an intensive six-week program, my husband and I had some serious sex. During that time, I zeroed in on every single thing I'd read that might help someone conceive a baby. I took vitamins and minerals until they were coming out of my ears, although I was told not to take too much vitamin E, which is especially bad if you have high blood pressure. I didn't have that problem.

My New York expert, Dr. Peller, told me I could take up to 10,000 milligrams of vitamin C without getting an upset stomach, especially if it was buffered. Cranberry juice was my drink of choice because of its natural antibodies. I also drank plenty of fresh water and applied the Edgar Cayce castor-oil pack to my abdomen.

In addition, I did body cleansings, I ate avocados and took bee pollen, which I read helped heal the female organs. I consumed "good" protein and exercised daily, including taking a long morning walk. I followed the late, great Max Gerson's instructions for a cleansing coffee enema and took steam baths to relax myself and rid my body of impurities. I ate foods that would help detox my body, strengthen my circulation, minimize infections and inflammation, balance the yin and yang, and nourish my female organs.

One of the biggest keys for me was meditation. I went beyond just a morning session of deep thinking and forced myself to think positive thoughts. *Positive, positive, positive.* It's very tough to do, but I tried to ignore negative thoughts and emotions. I needed to feed myself mentally, physically, and spiritually.

I did all of the above for this concentrated time period. About a month and a half later, I walked into the office of Dr. Charles Ledergerber, one of the most famous gynecologists in America, and the original doctor who told me that I had no hope of ever having another child. With a smile on my face, I said, "I think I'm pregnant."

He shook his head and sadly replied, "Oh, Diane, you can't be pregnant. I've told you it's impossible. Just go home and cry it out."

He had great empathy for my pain because he'd also lost a child. On that day, I looked him straight in the eyes and stated firmly, "Dr. Ledergerber, I *have* cried. Go do the test."

A few minutes later, he returned to the room with a shocked look on his face: The rabbit was in heaven. But my initial elation was deflated, because there was bad news along with the good. The doctor warned me that this might be another tubular pregnancy. I was told that I'd have to be monitored and watched very closely.

"It's not in the tube," I told him.

"Well, we have to be sure," he said.

Nine months later, I was on the table having a Cesarean because the doctors wanted to make sure that I had no complications. This precious daughter entered the world on February 10, 1967. After the baby was born, I remained on the table for four more hours while the doctors were busy removing 16 major adhesions caused by scar tissue wrapped around my female organs!

They didn't knock me out because I was told that when that's done, the patient bleeds more. So they gave me a spinal, and I just passed out. However, my subconscious mind heard one of the medical pros exclaim, "My God, my God! It's impossible that this child got through. This is a miracle!"

At that moment, my head popped up—which scared the heck out of the doctors. I slurred, "That's right, it's a miracle and a hell of a lot of hard work!" *Boom!* With those words, my head fell back and I passed out again.

I don't know how long it was until I came back to full consciousness after my surgery, but as soon as I opened my eyes, I asked, "Where's my baby?"

"Mrs. Dern, perhaps you want to wait until you're feeling better," the nurse said.

"Honey, bring me my baby," I demanded, like the lioness that's inside every woman.

The next moments weren't unlike those of any other mother on this earth who holds her child for the first time. As soon as they put her in my arms, tears sprang to my eyes. I'd never seen anything as beautiful in my entire life. Looking at my new and precious gift, I felt as if God were touching me. My daughter's celestial beauty entered every cell of my body, connecting me with the heavens, grounding me within the earth. That moment in time will forever be etched in my being. I named her Laura Elizabeth Dern.

When I think back on how I was never supposed to have another child, I sigh. I hurt for all the women out there who hear those words and then give up when they leave their doctor's office. Life is about determination. If someone tells you that you can't do something, maybe you can't . . . but then again, maybe you can. The point is that you don't have to subscribe to any prevailing story, however convincingly it's been told. With the help of God, you can write your own script, even if you're not a writer or an actress.

For proof, just take a look at my big picture. The script goes like this: I'm just a girl from Mississippi who at a young age takes off to become an actress, falls in love, gets married, has a beautiful baby, and then unfortunately suffers the loss of that beloved child. One day I say to God, "Please give me back a child, and I will use the talent You have given me to be a mirror for humanity, reflecting what's best and worst in all of us, and thus being of service to humankind as long as I live."

God not only answered my prayer, but He gave me the most beautiful daughter. This child decides, like her parents, to also become an actor. Of course I said, "No, no, no! Be a doctor, a lawyer, a housewife, a lepers' missionary—anything but an actress. It's too intangible!"

But mothers can never stop their children. Thank God she didn't listen, because she's also been given a gift. Not only did Laura Dern become an actress, but we ended up working together in director David Lynch's *Wild at Heart* and writer Calder Willingham's *Rambling Rose*. As fate would have it, we became the first mother and daughter to ever be nominated for Oscars in the same year and for the same film!

There are amazing spirals in all of our lives, some of which we recognize and some we don't. This was Laura's spiral and mine—and we touched it together.

The End of Our Marriage

Tragedy can sometimes pull a couple together, but if you're already fragmented in any way, it can tear you asunder. Bruce was a bad boy during our marriage, and this got worse after the tragedy. In many ways, Bruce was a man who wanted to hump the Western world. It wasn't for sex, it was simply for ego; it was less about the act of intercourse and more about loss.

You see, Bruce wasn't just an actor who faced rejection on a daily basis. He was a man who had lost a child, and he felt ripped apart at his core. What Bruce was doing with his extracurricular activities, on one level, had nothing to do with me. It was all about him trying to find himself. However, the impact of his actions on my life was immeasurable, because I valued loyalty and commitment.

At one point when we were temporarily separated and trying to find our way toward reconciliation, he was in Georgia filming *The Green Berets* with John Wayne. He made the mistake of allowing a girl whom he'd been up to his shenanigans with to come visit him on the set. More than just sensing something was wrong, I told Bruce that it was best that we got divorced.

Panicking, he professed his love and insisted that he couldn't live without me. I offered to join him immediately on the film set, but Bruce suddenly realized that the crew, who knew and liked me, would in all probability not hesitate to tell me about his extracurricular activities.

Terrified, he went to the great John Wayne to beg out of his role. They'd already shot a scene with him, and it would cost the company quite a bit of money to replace Bruce. But Wayne, in his inimitable style, immediately agreed to let him go. "Son," the Duke told him, "you can always get another part. But you might not be able to find another woman you really love. Go home, boy."

But there was no home left, and there would be no reunion. Too much had happened, and the chasm was too wide. We just couldn't find our way back to each other again.

Many people who get divorced want to tear their former mate apart. If you have children together and hold this anger and hatred within, then it's *you* who will pay through the nose for those emotions, and it's your child who will take the arrows aimed at your ex. If you hurt the parent of your child, then your own little one will suffer. Ask yourself: *Why would I hurt the person I love the most—my child?*

During our divorce, I didn't hate Bruce, nor did I want him to be destroyed. I longed for my child's father to become as great a man as possible. This wasn't only for him, but for our daughter and me. Bruce Dern had fathered my two children, and that bond would always be there . . . well . . . maybe not.

CHAPTER 3

MY SCHOOL OF PARENTING

One of my theories in life is that we have to be solid enough to provide a foundation so that our children can stand on our shoulders in the hopes that they'll see further than we did. If that happens, then the entire human race might really become humane—that's the hope.

I was a single mother back in the days when there weren't many of us around. Most women I knew were married with kids; I just had the child but lost the ring. When I look back now, I'm not sure how I raised a daughter on my own *and* worked at an acting career.

Let's take a moment and sing the praises of all the single working mothers out there. They don't call it a mother lode for nothing, because this type of life can be a *real* load. Today there are many single fathers out there, and my hat is also off to them.

I did take child support from Bruce, which was basically whatever he could afford that month. He came through and paid, but I didn't ask for as much as he could afford, due to my lack of cleverness. I only took alimony for a short time, and I took less than was appropriate. Don't be stupid, ladies: Take the money. Pride goeth before the fall.

I had pride, fell, and was left with a horrendous financial struggle. In fact, years later Bruce was living in a multimillion-dollar home on the beach, and I was in a little apartment outside Hollywood with our daughter. That's just not right. I call my choice "the leftover residual from ego." However, I did take enough money to pay for a therapist so I could try to get myself balanced.

I also did a few not-so-sane things at the time. When I first divorced Bruce, I bought him a beautiful blue suit, because he has beautiful blue eyes. The outfit was to help him go out there and attract the ladies—it was my ironic parting gift to my husband. Of course, he didn't need any help finding women, which was one of the reasons we got divorced.

How dumb could this Mississippi blonde have been in those days? Actually, I wasn't dumb at all, just young, confused, and emotionally ragged. I was in the total spiral of emotions, and I wasn't thinking clearly. I'd like to say that both men and women shouldn't put themselves down for being stupid while they're going through a crisis. We're all foolish to a certain degree—it's called being human.

Meanwhile, I was lucky enough to have my own mother, Mary, there to help me. However, it was difficult for mother and me to live together because, being a Leo, my mom carried a kind of subtle but overpowering energy, which clashed at times with my own fire. I'm an outgoing Sagittarian, but my mother was a passive aggressor and a lot stronger.

For instance, if she was getting ready to fire you from a job, well, you were f-i-r-e-d, packed up, and in your car driving away before you knew what hit you. On the other hand, I'd have to say it about five times out loud before I could really fire someone, and then I'd ask them if they wouldn't mind leaving.

But giving birth and raising your own child opens the door to forgiveness for the weakness and mistakes made by your own parents. My mother was also gentle, lovely, and just about the most wonderful grandmother on this planet. When she was with Laura, my child's eyes would light up because she was that happy. The two of them developed a deep bond, and I hope that I have that someday with my own grandchildren.

The Hawaiians believe that the grandmother holds the original creation of the grandchild in her body—holding the link and lineage through time. It's her obligation and privilege to provide a presence that opens the heart of the grandchild, thereby enlarging her own in turn. This fulfills the spiral.

God gave me talent, intelligence, and strength. Most people misjudge strong women by defining their power as manipulative, cold, cunning, and invulnerable. There's an error in this reasoning, and it's far from true. Strength at its center is pliable, soft, and receptive.

Most of the legendary actresses I've had the privilege to know and work with—Maureen Stapleton, Shelley Winters, Bette Davis, Barbara Stanwyck, Lainie Kazan, Renée Taylor, and Connie Stevens, among many—are strong women. I always found that the ones who are the toughest on the outside are the most vulnerable on the inside, and they're also the most trustworthy. I hope that I'm that kind of woman, too.

I never liked the cool, clever actresses who'd greet me with a smile and a warm hello in the morning, only to zing me behind my back with unsheathed claws. They were sweet to my face, but devious game players behind my back. I'll take shoot-from-the-hip emotional honesty any day over a pleasant backstabber, which brings me back to my post-divorce economics.

I took any job I could to pay the rent, not thinking of the consequences or really building a career. Meanwhile, my ex-husband kept climbing. Was I bitter about it? Well, I tried to do what I like to call "keeping my pants clean." I'd pray, "Let me do the good deed while I can today." In other words, I tried to keep things positive between my ex and me. I tried not to be bitter about what I perceived as the huge inequalities between our respective standards of living.

It's so important to let go of resentment, because in the future you might miss out on an opportunity, and closed doors *never* facilitate opportunity. For instance, many years later I directed Bruce in a film called *Mrs. Munck*. In fact, I was the first woman in history to direct her ex-husband in a movie. Ladies, if you want revenge, direct your ex—just kidding! I'll never forget the day when I told him, "My God, you're one of the most magnificent actors I've ever been privileged to work with—but you were a terrible husband!" He laughed, and we hugged.

Bruce came from a prominent family, starting with the fact that his uncle was poet laureate Archibald MacLeish. His grandfather George Henry Dern was the first non-Mormon governor of Utah and was chosen to be the Secretary of War under Franklin D. Roosevelt. Even though Bruce's immediate family is made up of staunch Republicans, his godfather was Adlai Stevenson, a Democratic candidate for the presidency.

Success is wonderful, but money can't buy everything. When Laura was a little girl, I was doing the hit play *A Texas Trilogy: LuAnn Hampton Laverty Oberlander* at the Kennedy Center's Eisenhower Theater. Even though Bruce's family had actually served in the White House, this country girl was so thrilled to be the first one to take our ten-year-old daughter for a private grand tour of that fabulous institution. We waltzed into the Gerald Ford White House and I heard the words "Miss Ladd and Laura, welcome." Whoooohooooooo!

Parenting Lessons

The first lesson I learned as a single parent of a daughter is that you have to let each other off the hook. If you make somebody feel guilty, they're going to hate you. Guilt and resentment are entwined as a kind of negative pas de deux. (By the way, you shouldn't make adults feel guilty either.)

As for kids, relating to them at their level of emotional development makes for validated children. Talking down to a child is patronizing and can lead to feelings of inferiority. You can treat them in a childlike way, but not childishly. The latter comes with all kinds of judgments.

In terms of structure and discipline, let's say that your son or daughter does something wrong, which everyone will do from time to time. Rather than using the old paradigm of strident authority and fear-based parenting, let the child off the hook by creating an emotion based in safety and truth. It's a unique way of parenting: Let things slide once in a while—not all the time, but every now and then.

When my little girl did something a little naughty, I didn't jump to the age-old "Go to your room!" Instead, I'd look at her and say, "All right, here's what we're gonna do: We're gonna go out and have a malted milk and talk about this." I guarantee that your child's jaw will hit the floor—and he or she will listen!

Understand that you're not encouraging improper behavior. You just go get the malt and say, "I thought it would be a good thing if we shared something sweet while we talked. I'm not giving you the malt because you did something wrong. And, by the way, because you did something wrong, you can't go to a movie this weekend."

I never ended the talk on a negative note. I'd always add, "But, honey, I want you to know that you're loved. I also want you to know that we all do things wrong. I want to help you do things *right.* And if you don't understand what to do, just talk to me. Talk to me, baby. Use your words." At this point, if you're using this strategy, you'll put your arms around your child and hug him. That way the kid isn't afraid to come and tell you that he did something wrong.

It's sad that many parents take the opposite approach. They wait at the kitchen table for their child to return home and bark, "Get your butt over here! You did something horrible!" I think that I've figured out why certain folks do that: They're still terrified of their own parents, and they remain scared of their own childhoods. As kids, these people were told that they didn't do things right. Now, as grown-ups, they're so afraid of making a mistake—and God forbid that their child should make one!

It's tragic to me when I run into people who were abused either physically or emotionally as children. Just so you're aware, there are approximately 374,270 registered child molesters of children living in the United States today. *Beware!* Protect your child. The parents of these criminals didn't love themselves either and took that loathing to a state where they abused their own children in one way or another. The cycle can continue generation after generation.

I'm certainly not saying that I'm a perfect parent. I don't believe that anyone fits that description, just as there aren't any perfect people yet! God isn't finished with us, and we're all still evolving or spiraling. I made a lot of mistakes as a mother, and my daughter will mess up, and my grandchildren will do the same with their children. What's important is to be able to say that you really tried.

The other day someone asked me if I believed in spanking. I can see how a parent might be caught in the type of emotional spiral where they believe that it's time to go to the last resort, which is to get physical. However, I don't believe that "to spare the rod is to spoil the child." No way! I just don't believe in hitting, which is basically physical abuse. Talk it out, even when you don't think the words are working. They'll get through eventually, and you'll be glad that you didn't go down that other path.

Healthy Parenting

It's important to listen to your child with the "ear" of your heart because it creates mutual self-respect. I tried to really hear my daughter, encouraging her to feel that she would always be safe coming to me to talk about anything. I'll never forget the afternoon when Laura was 13 and came home from school, put her books down, grabbed some ice cream, and calmly stated, "You know, Mother, a lot of kids in my class have already had sex."

This utterly shocked, nearly hysterical mother froze on the outside. Inside, a rapidly pounding heart silently shook my entire body. But forcing myself to be calm and rational, I asked in a quiet voice, "Well, honey, how do you feel about that?"

My daughter took several bites of her ice cream, sighed, and responded with the wisdom that God gives the innocent. "Well, even though their bodies may be ready for sex, emotionally they're not prepared to exchange energy with another human being."

I was stunned and thought, *If only we could teach all of our children the meaning of that statement, then this would be a better world.* The point is that we must show our children how to make choices that are good for them and will bring the results that they really want—not just provide a momentary pleasure that might complicate their lives. It's still a good idea to teach looking before leaping. (I wish I could get that one through to a few adults, too!)

On that day over ice cream, I said to my wise daughter, "That's really a mature opinion, Laura. I'm so impressed with your point of view." She grinned happily, made some popcorn, and went to get the checkers game. Discussion over.

PART II

How to Help Yourself

RELEASING ANGER

Anger is one of the most dangerous emotions that we experience as human beings. It makes us extremely uneasy—leading to a state of "dis-ease"—which often causes depression. Doctors have proven that when the body's depressed, it sets up an excess of what are called free radicals . . . which create disease. There are many theories regarding free radicals, and some doctors are even of the opinion that these suckers can mutilate and deplete the oxygen within our cells.

Negativity will make you sick, and there are no ifs, ands, or buts about it; anger is like a big black hole. This state of being sets off free radicals and can cause cancer, which is a medically proven fact. Sure, cancer might be inherited and in your DNA, but how can one person who has this road map get sick but her sibling won't?

There's a woman I know whose husband was running around on her. She caught him and was heartbroken, crying to me on the phone, "Diane, I'm just not going to *give* anymore!" Well, the kidneys represent the giving glands in the body (in the female, it's the kidneys and breasts). So my friend put up a lock that became a block, which can often manifest into a knot. Whether that snarl is a cyst or a tumor depends on an individual's makeup. This woman did develop the knot, and unfortunately it was a tumor that became malignant. You see,

I believe that if you go around all day thinking that the world has done you wrong, you make yourself sick.

On the other hand, I've seen people cured of cancer by releasing their anger. Healers will use hypnosis, physical therapy, and mental programming to help patients, and by loving yourself, you'll release rage. I try to meditate every morning before starting the day's activities to rid myself of any irritation. If I get lazy and think, *Oh, I'm late—I can't meditate right now,* then I'll usually have a less-than-perfect day.

So many people seem to be saying, "Gotta go, gotta go, gotta go!" There's no stopping to check in with themselves . . . no stopping to breathe. It's a tough way to live and a poor way to set energy into motion.

Your job is to jump-start your energy in a positive mode. Your body will heal things inside for you if you follow this advice. If your energy is in a better place, then you'll have an improved, healthier life.

The Man Who Released Anger

About two decades ago, I met a man while I was lecturing at San Diego State University, and I ended up being engaged to him for six years. He was a diplomate on the American Board of Family Practice and lectured all over, including at Harvard and at the Congress of Science and Religion in Rome, Italy. His clinic was in Florida, and I spent a lot of time down there when I wasn't working on movies.

I met so many women with breast cancer during that time, and they hadn't trusted the doctors who just wanted to take their breasts off. All these ladies somehow found their way to this doctor and his clinic. He'd help them restore the balance within their bodies through many methods, such as physical chelation (a way to cleanse your system); a proper diet (including herbs, vitamins, and minerals); hypnosis; mind programming; massage; yoga; detoxing; and other medical and alternative-modality treatments.

All of my fiancé's patients were facing their own version of darkness: Some of them talked about mates who'd died or rejected them and left; others reported dysfunctional relationships with husbands, parents, lovers, partners, and/or children who'd disappointed them or left. These women had a right to be angry, but they also had a right to live. So to survive, they needed to purge the madness.

Everybody reading this book needs to know just one thing: I saw miracles. This was in the mid-'80s and it was "lightbulb time." God was right there, helping, healing, and creating "aha" moments every single day.

My fiancé worked with his patients by teaching them to release their negative energy and anger. When most of these women would go back to their primary caregivers, there was no cancer in their bodies. None! I know that it was the power of the mind; I firmly believe that the cells lock up and stop getting oxygen when we're upset all the time.

Anger is one of the most destructive forces in our lives because it blocks and then sickens us. The sad thing is that we get angry every single day of our lives. I'm always preaching about this subject to the extent that my friends tease me, saying, "Diane, if the master Jesus hadn't gotten angry that time in the temple and expressed it by throwing that table . . . why, you might not have had anything to do with him!"

"Well," I reply, "of course I would. It just might be a different story."

What we need to remember, however, is that after Jesus expressed his justifiable anger by demonstrating that those who were committing such evil deeds were wrong, he simply went on his way and didn't dwell on it, preach about it, or internalize it. He left the sinners to wallow in their own squalor, learn their own lessons, and deal with their personal karma. So take a lesson from Jesus.

Many people love to be angry because they're hooked on the drama of it. They don't know if there's anything else in their lives to replace that. Holding on to—or even conjuring up—all that rage is really a cry for attention. Nearly all of us do it at times.

These days there are so many places to turn to rid yourself of this emotion and to get help for your problems. My fiancé was one of the great, humble, and dedicated physicians who helped found the American Holistic Medical Association (AHMA). These are doctors who do not reject traditional medicine, but believe in the inclusiveness of alternative modalities. In other words, they refuse to throw the baby out with the bathwater.

My advice is this: You have to let go, detox, cleanse out your body, and circulate positive energy. You can even do a colonic or a wheatgrass or coffee enema. (If you're unfamiliar with these practices, please go visit a professional in these fields.)

We should all try simply loving ourselves again, since that's what healed those cancer patients most of all. Try to push away the negativity in your mind; give yourself a vacation from it. Do it for just one day and see how much better you feel physically.

The worst kind of anger comes from fighting with your family. If you can stop that, then I suggest that you do so for your own health. A family is a special kind of spiral: They're your loved ones, and you run in circles with them. This is close to your own soul and connects you with other spirits and to each other throughout time. Family is the great circling hoop of connection.

Just about every member of nearly all families is dysfunctional in some way. If we can see the craziness in each other and detach, respect, and even forgive, it helps us evolve. But sometimes you do have to separate yourself from your relatives if they're creating bad karma in your life.

There are people who abuse their own mates, children, and other loved ones. Those family members are ill and are often caught up in some form of mental, emotional, or physical addiction. They dump anger on others and refuse to take responsibility for their lives and actions. It's important that we know who can be helped through compassion and understanding, and that we recognize that there are others whom we need to have distance from. Sometimes the only solution is simply separation.

I know people who've been abused but still try to see that their abuser gets some help—this is called "sending back the good." Of course I don't advise doing this if it involves endangering your own psyche or physical being. It's a miracle, however, if you've been hurt and want to help someone who's wronged you. Forgiveness and action are powerful when working together. I think that this is the most wonderful example of moving inward, upward, and toward the best you can be as a person.

Sometimes, however, I see people acting too quickly. They write off loved ones and family members for the smallest infractions. Family, like the land, is very important. These people are a part of us, and even if we think that they're crazy, we shouldn't ignore them. If we knew the personal details of anybody else's family, we'd consider them certifiable, too. Each of us holds our own landscape—bone, blood, and water. We create this DNA over and over on this earth.

Be aware that family members who are insecure will often externalize it, dumping what feels unwanted onto another person for them to hold or carry. I believe that we must suck up our own fragmented parts, heal our hurts, be gentle with what's still unfinished in ourselves, and extend compassion and kindness to others. Don't you think that the world would be better if we all did that?

Those who are insecure will sometimes pick one person and make their life hell; it's another form of abuse. A guy who's a coward will go into his office and take all kinds of what I call "manure jazz" from his boss. Then he'll come home and take it out on his wife and children, since it's the only way he can make himself feel important. That's a terrible tragedy, and in fact, this man is missing an opportunity for real love at home. (But don't let me just place it on the male gender—many women do the same thing. And in the animal kingdom, females are often the worst aggressors.)

Why can't we just stop the anger spiral and have equality, fun, love, supportiveness, growth, and joy? That's a much more rewarding way to live. It's the same with the greater family of humanity: I'd love to see all the countries stop this stupid bickering. Wouldn't you like the terrorists to stop their insanity? The politicians should also quit playing their games, as should the doctors, lawyers, and everyone else.

But it all starts with the individual. If each of us put out the fires of our own anger, then we as members of individual tribes and countries wouldn't be motivated to perpetuate wars. It would be a much healthier, less angry world. Is this too simple for anyone to hear and understand?

So what can you do if you find yourself getting into anger mode? Initially, you need to put out the heat by walking away from the situation, reconnecting with yourself, moving your body, and hitting or screaming into a pillow. You can be with your emotions in a way that's neither acting them out nor repressing it. The next step is to understand what created the anger: insecurity or fear, or sometimes you're just plain tired. Ask yourself: *What do I need? What's the anger telling me?* These are good questions to answer after you come back to yourself.

It's the cleansing, flushing out, and letting go of negative energy that clears the mind and allows that healing power of spiritual energy, which brings you joy and even physical health. When you hold on to rage, you hurt yourself; when you forgive someone else or yourself and let it go, you're only doing yourself a favor. So let go of the mistakes you've made, be proud of what you've accomplished, and be proud of yourself as a human being.

The good news is that just one person handling the hot potato of their anger and transforming it can change everything. I'm working hard on my own sometimes-formidable anger. Will you join me? We need to do it right now because our world depends on us. Try simply saying "Thank you" when someone holds a door open, and you'll start a spiraling circle of loving energy. Do it right now.

I know a young woman who's working hard as a writer and is the mother of a two-year-old son. She feels that she can't do anything right because she works long hours and then tries to cram in as much parenting time at night with her little boy as possible. He's a cranky type of kid who pitches a doozy of a fit before going to sleep, and my friend chalks this up to her failure as a mother.

She feels the way a lot of young women do these days: They've decided that they're not doing right by their jobs, children, or husbands. But she has to step back and realize one thing: She isn't perfect. Before all of you young working moms blow apart, you need to slow down for a day or two, ask for some help, and do something for yourself, such as having lunch with a girlfriend. I know that this sounds like an easy solution, but the point is that *anyone* who's overwhelmed needs to do something to reinforce herself. A manicure or a day at the mall does wonders, and so does a little therapy.

Parents can also get professional help. I know that this doesn't sound possible when you're barely paying for your apartment and have a screaming kid who's keeping you from sleeping. But you can go to a church or community organization to get assistance; you don't have to beg or borrow for this aid. Just say, "I need to have support because I can't handle it alone. In God's name, help me."

If you ask a charity or religious community for help, you'll most likely get it. The trick is to create a strong support structure—a link of community resources and friendships—that you can depend on. Don't wait or be so proud that you won't allow yourself to see the problem until it balloons and festers. Everyone needs a hand in some way at every moment; life is about finding the help you need and making the best choices to enrich the lives for you and your loved ones.

Feeling Overwhelmed?

When it comes to therapy, there used to be a taboo about asking for this type of help, which always struck me as nonsense. We can get the car repaired, and there's no stigma; we can replace the bottom stair that's worn out, and nobody says a word. Everyone knows the importance of setting a broken arm. Why in God's name would anyone feel that there's anything wrong with getting a little help to have the mind fixed?

Honey, your mind is the big machine running it all. You don't think you need a little extra oil in there sometimes? Why not get a professional? I know, I know: You can talk to a friend. That can be good, but there are times when you need someone who has a degree.

Would you let the mechanic teach your child's first-grade class? Would you let the teacher fix your car? The answer is no! Of course, there are good and bad mechanics, and the same thing goes for psychiatrists: You'll find excellent ones out there, and others whom I wouldn't let advise my dog.

I've always said, "If you have a problem, find the right therapist." This includes marriage or parent-child counselors. Today, if you can't afford to see someone in private practice, hospitals have group sessions and access to other professionals who don't charge a lot of money, but do a world of good.

Years ago I went to the UCLA Medical Center because I was overloaded and needed a little bit of support. I was a single mother who wasn't doing a lot of acting at the time, and I didn't have very much money to get myself some help. So I decided to go to this facility where, for seven dollars a week, I could go to therapy.

I'll never forget walking into my counselor's office on the first day wondering what my seven bucks would buy me. Inside, I found a Japanese gentleman who weighed about 350 pounds. The first words out of his mouth were, "What movie stars do you know?" This was my therapist, and depression quickly set in.

I could have been paying this guy $150 a week, and he still would have been asking the same inappropriate questions.

Quality doesn't always go hand in hand with the amount of money you pay for something. A very astute person once said, "Buy the best and you only cry once." I believe in karma, fate, and guardian angels; I also firmly believe in the good sense to make decisions that are good for you. I found a better therapist and for the same money at UCLA. It follows that if you need help, and you ask God and the Universe for it, you might get better assistance than someone who whips out his American Express Platinum Card. Again, my motto is: *Have a little faith, kick a little dirt.*

CHAPTER 5

AND NOW FOR SOME GOOD OLD-FASHIONED HEALING

Years ago, I had the great fortune of becoming good friends with Johnny and June Carter Cash, who were two of the most beautiful people to ever grace this planet. Let me just say that they were kind, smart, talented, and loving human beings. They were also an amazing couple, and I observed their love firsthand in 1978 when I did a TV movie with them called *Thaddeus Rose and Eddie.*

We shot it in Texas, and I'll never forget that Johnny, June, and I saved all the local stray animals we could, including finding families for every lost dog we could spot on the plains. Johnny could also make a mean vegan chili. "I'm not a big meat eater, Diane," he told me. "When I eat meat, my muscles get weak." We all became fast friends and discussed our pasts, including my background in Mississippi and my views on metaphysics.

Several years later, one night out of the blue, their daughter Rosanne Cash phoned me and said, "Daddy's in the hospital, and he's very ill, Diane. The doctors say that he won't make it past Friday. Mother wants to talk to you—please call her at the hospital." Then she gave me a private phone number.

I dialed it quickly and immediately said, "I want to give Johnny a present, June. I want to give him a healing." June was a great lady, but she was also, of course, a concerned one. I'm not sure if she knew what kind of procedure I was thinking of for her precious Johnny, who by this time was in serious condition.

Stopping me mid-sentence, June said, "Now, Diane, you know that Johnny and I are both Bible people!"

"Oh well, June . . . I sure am glad that you weren't on the planet the same time as Jesus," I replied.

What followed was one of those awkward pauses. Then she asked, "What do you mean by that?"

"You would have been so busy telling Jesus who he could and couldn't heal that nobody would have gotten any help!"

I could hear June laugh on the other end of the phone, which was what I wanted. "All right, all right, Diane," she said. "We'll take the healing. What is it? It better not be strange or anything!"

I told her about a special friend of mine who was a great healer and worked with medical doctors in hospitals. He was also a leading teacher at Healing Touch International (HTI).

June said, "Don't tell me all this! I'm frantic about Johnny, so just tell me what you're gonna do."

"Steve Anderson is his name. He's a male nurse and a retired lieutenant commander in the Navy," I explained. "He used to think healing was a bunch of bunk until his superior officer made him attend a lecture. He became intrigued when he discovered that he had this great healing power, and he's been helping the world ever since."

The Cashes immediately decided to make an appointment with this man who could do his work from 3,000 miles away. In his mind's eye, he could run his hands through your energy and "see" your body. Some healers can do that, but I can't. (I wish I could!) So I called my friend and said, "I want to give Johnny Cash a healing." He agreed to a call the next night at 8 P.M.

Steve called on Tuesday night, and June put him on the phone with Johnny, who was gravely ill. You see, the deal is that the healer has to ask permission first before any work can begin. "Mr. Cash, Diane Ladd has arranged for me to give you some healing energy. May I do that?" Steve asked.

Johnny, who was always such a gentleman, replied, "Well, I'd be mighty appreciative, sir. What do I have to do?"

"Just lie back and relax," Steve instructed . . . and three days later, Johnny left the hospital, flew to New York, and did a live concert that same night.

A few months after this, I went to Johnny and June's home for a big party following an amazing concert from the "Man in Black." He hugged me and thanked me for helping him.

"Diane, I thank you, too. I think it really helped him," June told me.

"It was a gift from God," I said. She still wasn't so convinced when it came to alternative healing, but I could tell that she could live with the idea of a gift from the Heavenly Father. After all, she was a Bible person.

A Little Piece of Rock

Rock Hudson and I had some kind of karmic connection. What can I say about him, except that he was drop-dead gorgeous? He was also a perfect gentleman and one of the kindest men I ever met. I told him a story one time about how when Bruce Dern and Bette Davis were filming *Hush, Hush, Sweet Charlotte,* Bette threw a party, but first loaded all her guests on a bus and took them to the famous Schwab's drugstore. After I related this tale, Rock rented a bus, threw a party, and took all of us to a fancy restaurant and then to his house.

In the middle of the festivities, Rock and I were sitting on a couch just talking to each other. There was another man (who someone later told me was Rock's lover), and he kept giving me the evil eye. This very jealous young man said, "Diane, how would you like a drink?"

I nodded while I continued talking to Rock. It wasn't just friendship between the two of us; observers couldn't help but notice that something electric was going on. Yes, he was gay, but several people told me that as a younger man, he'd had a long affair with an actress named Marilyn Maxwell . . . and everyone said that I looked like her.

Rock insisted on taking me home later that night. At the door, I stared into his gorgeous face, he looked deeply into my eyes . . . and then I clutched my stomach and gasped, "Rock, I'm sorry, but I have to go in right away because I'm sick!"

I barely made it through the door and passed out from my one drink, which Rock's friend had obviously laced with something. The next day, I called my doctor and explained my symptoms.

"Somebody clearly slipped you a mickey," the doc confirmed.

In spite of this incident, the platonic friendship between Rock and me survived, and we had a lot of fun over the years. It endured until the end: When he was on his deathbed, a producer who'd worked with him on most of his Doris Day movies called me and said, "Diane, Rock really needs you."

"Oh, please, take me to him. I can give him some healing," I responded before I could think twice—and that did it. The producer never called again, and later, he refused to take me to see my friend. I wondered why the idea of a healing panicked him. Did he think that I'd be chanting or doing weird things?

I learned much later that just prior to my conversation with this producer, another friend—a very famous singer and actor—had visited Rock. This person declared, "You're a sinner! You have to repent and come to Jesus now to save your soul or you'll burn in hell!"

Oh God . . . I guess this poor producer thought that I'd do something like that, so that's why he wouldn't let me see Rock. It was a shame, because I really wanted to connect with him again before he died. While my wonderful pal Johnny Cash was fortunately given the opportunity to accept the healing, this other beloved friend, actor, and legend wasn't given the choice because his people didn't allow it.

I still miss him, and he remains one of the most gorgeous men—gay or straight—who ever passed through Hollywood. I'll never forget all the good times with this sensitive person who brought so much laughter to our world. It was my good fortune to know this wonderful man.

Healing and Me

As for me . . . well folks, I'm a healing junkie. I'll never forget the first time I went for a healing. It was with a man named Doug Johnson, who has since passed away, but was a very famous practitioner who came with many recommendations. To find someone for yourself, ask other people. It's a good way to "out" the phonies—and there are many of them, so please *be very careful.*

I remember talking to my friend Jess Stearn, a very well-known newspaper reporter and author. He'd gone to Doug himself, despite some family members insisting that it was all a bunch of baloney. Jess's relative was a very famous medical doctor who was coping with the sad fact that his ten-year-old son had a serious health problem. It was heartbreaking, because the family had been told that there was absolutely no hope.

In my book, there's *always* hope, and Jess felt the same way, too. He'd heard about Doug and begged him to help the boy. By the grace of God, the boy's father decided to look into alternative methods, and allowed Jess to take the child to Doug for a healing. The young lad not only survived, but today he's a beautiful young man.

I must take a moment here to say a little more about Doug, who was a funny guy and very Truman Capote–like in his mannerisms. He had a heart murmur that was diagnosed when he was 12, resulting in his visiting just about every doctor's office around, and when he was only eighteen after visiting the Mayo Clinic, where they told his parents, "We're very sorry, but your son will be dead in three months. There's absolutely no hope."

But Doug didn't die. Instead, he decided to try to heal himself, since he'd heard about it as a little boy . . . and he lived to be 77 years old. To say that he was blessed with special extras is an understatement. He often spoke of having visions of angels who came to him, including the angel of his own mother. Sometimes, if somebody had just died, they'd appear to him, too.

He was a gentle, funny, very sane, logical guy. People came from all over Europe and parts of Asia to be healed by him, and I even brought my Laura to him when she was sick. At that same time, I happened to be getting the flu. Doug gave me a quick healing that day and *Pow!*—it was so strong that it knocked the illness right out of me.

As an aside, my mother was also suffering with the flu around the same time, and I took her to Doug. Naturally, she said, "Where is my crazy daughter taking me? There isn't anything to that, Diane. There isn't anything! It's probably the work of the devil!"

"Stop it, Mary. Come on and meet the man, for God's sake!" I insisted. And after an hour of treatment, the woman who'd been sick to her stomach for days said, "Diane, aren't you gonna take me out to eat? I'm starving!"

So I took her to Lawry's steak house, where she was wilder than a mad hatter! My senior-citizen mother was giggly, silly, and even playfully threw a piece of bread at somebody. I think she OD'd on the energy given to her that day, and I joked with her: "I'm never gonna take you for a healing again." This gentle little Southern lady was like a child on too much sugar. I guess she finally experienced what I'd known for a long time: When it comes to healing, there *is* something to it!

These days I often rely on healer Steve Anderson, the man who helped my friend Johnny Cash. In 2005, I had some very painful work done on my mouth after cracking a tooth. It was the beginning of a nightmare: The dentist had to do a root canal on one tooth and then two implants on the other side of my aching mouth.

One thing led to another, and suddenly I needed to go in for a dental operation where they had to administer anesthesia. It was supposed to be a four-hour procedure, but turned into a ten-hour extravaganza—followed by the suggestion to put temporary caps on some of my teeth. I was told that I should have another dose of anesthesia to get this done.

I didn't want to put those chemicals into my body again unless I had to, because I knew how toxic they were. So I called Steve and said, "Listen, I'm going to call you when I sit down in the dentist's chair, and I want you zapping me with healing. At the same time, I'll try to do a little self-hypnosis."

He did his job, and I made it through the entire ordeal without any anesthetic. My mouth got stretched and tired, but I wasn't in agonizing pain. My doctor even said, "You're the only person I've ever seen do this. It's amazing." Uh-huh.

I have to tell you one more little story before we leave this topic. When Laura was a little girl, she went to a Catholic school in Beverly Hills. One sunny spring morning, the nuns asked the children to share something for show and tell. Well, Laura told the class about healers . . . and the nuns went bonkers!

"That's heathen!" one of the teachers boomed. "Anybody doing healing is a phony."

My little eight-year-old sprite of a daughter just put her hands on her tiny hips and held her ground. "Healers help people," she informed the class.

At that, the nuns went lunatic crazy: "Healers are going to hell!" one yelled to the class. And then she scolded my daughter: "Miss Laura Dern, don't you dare come in here and talk about things like astrology and healing."

The next day, I got myself right in front of that nun. "Sister," I said softly, "hello! It's so lovely to be in your classroom." She stood there frowning at me, but I wouldn't be deterred. "I know that my daughter misunderstood you," I continued, "and I want you to explain something very important to her, if you would be so kind."

The nun looked a little less hostile, so I kept on going. "As we both know, little children's minds are so impressionable," I said. The nun nodded in agreement, and at that point I knew that she was ready to listen to what I'd really come to tell her.

"I know that Laura was talking about healing, and she told me that you, her teacher, said healing was wrong." The woman began to speak, but I soldiered on. "But honey, I must have totally misunderstood what Laura was telling me. As you and I both know, the master Jesus was one of the top healer of all time."

The teacher's mouth dropped open.

"Come on," I added. "The Catholic church is based on

Jesus's healings, and he had 12 disciples. They all had different gifts: One was a leader, one was a loyal friend, one was a little psychic, one was a healer, one was a little bit of this, and one was a little bit of that. Jesus cured men and made them walk. He healed the blind and said, 'What I do, you can do in my name.' Isn't it possible that Jesus could be working through others in our world today?'

The nun took one hand and touched her heart.

"Darlin,'" I asked her, "would you please explain all that to my precious Laura and maybe the rest of the class when you get a chance?"

This woman's mouth was agape, and in a nervous voice she replied, "Oh yes, absolutely yes, Miss Ladd. Jesus *was* a healer. I'll explain it to Laura—I'll tell everyone."

"You have a wonderful day! Bye-bye now," I replied. With that, my job there was finished. I went on my way, and the class learned about Jesus and his many healing talents. I was grateful that I'd found the words to heal a few closed minds.

By the way, I wouldn't get my master's in psychology until much later, but I knew that I couldn't blast into that school and yell at the officials. The first lesson of psychology is that if you make somebody feel guilty, they're going to hate you, as I mentioned earlier. Guilt and resentment are inexplicably intertwined.

STAYING HEALTHY

When I was a child, I was at death's door with a bad bout of pneumonia. I was this sweaty little thing, lying there in my feverish delirium and screaming, "Vanilla, vanilla!" Don't ask me why I wanted vanilla; I guess I was just hysterical with sickness.

My father, who was out of town at that time, and who was intuitive, came home and rushed in the door and asking, "Where's my little sick baby?"

"Daddy, vanilla, vanilla," I moaned when I saw his form in the my bedroom doorway.

"My baby wants a banana split," he said, ignoring the fact that I had a 102-degree fever.

I don't know if it's a medically proven remedy, but that banana split not only calmed me, but my fever also went down very shortly afterward and I was on the road to recovery. I'm not prescribing ice-cream treats for all that ails us, but what the hey—they can't hurt, right? Honestly, I think that it was the loving care of my father that cured me.

When I was about ten, I squeezed a pimple on my hand and ended up getting blood poisoning. The blood streak was about half an inch wide and about half an inch below my shoulder. This is a very dangerous thing, because the poison can go right to your heart and kill you.

My parents quickly gave me penicillin and sulfa drugs. The country doctor even came and looked at the streak, which was a stubborn one that wasn't going away. "If it goes up another half inch, we'll have to amputate her arm," he reported.

To add to my woes, I had an allergic reaction. The doctor wanted to take me off the sulfa and keep me on the penicillin, but my parents refused to take me off the sulfa. That was the drug that saved my arm, and my father somehow knew that it would do the trick. How easy it would have been for him to just listen to the doctor and not question his advice. I'm thankful that Daddy had a few questions in his mind.

Those were my two worst health problems as a young girl. It's a miracle that there weren't bigger issues because I ate the way that Southerners did back then, which meant a steady diet of too much fat and too many carbs. As a child, however, I didn't want to eat meat. My father would put it on the table, but I had no interest in that cute little cow that could have been a pet. Daddy was livid because it cost so much.

"Girl, I work hard. Eat your meat," he'd say.

So I'd chew it up and then spit it into my napkin. Whooooeee, he'd get mad!

"You swallow that meat, girl! Your daddy worked hard to put that on the table!" he'd yell. "It's good stuff for your bones—you eat that meat."

I guess in those days no one knew about "blood-type A" foods, which means that I'm inclined to eat more vegetables, and it wasn't common knowledge that red meat pretty much clogs up your heart and ruins your kidneys. The culture didn't encourage us to listen to our body in order to stay healthy. Today, I eat a lot of vegetables and fish, while only sometimes having the food that my Daddy loved so much.

The fact is that when I was a young actress living in New York City, I couldn't afford any meat. (I guess Daddy was right about certain things!) I didn't have money for vitamins either, but no one cared about them at the time. I didn't get into them until I started having children. In fact, they helped get me pregnant, although my doctor still says, "Vitamins don't make babies."

My reply is: "That's what you think!"

It wasn't long ago that I had a liver scan. The doctor actually looked at the results while I was still lying on his table, and he even called his associates over to see. At first I got a little scared, but then I heard him say, "My God, this woman has the liver of a 25-year-old." I didn't dare tell him that it's because I do a coffee enema every six months to clean out my liver.

Exercise, another important part of staying healthy, has always been important in my life. When I was a young actress making the rounds in New York City, I didn't need a gym. I walked miles every single day and was in the best shape of my life. Then I did a dance act when I was about 18 that also kept me in tip-top shape, since it meant 346 kicks a night. I cried when I had to do it, but it established a foundation of fitness still present in my now-older body, which is doing pretty well, thank you very much.

Exercise is a wonderful thing, even though I'm not always wild about it. It isn't the most thrilling part of the day, but it *is* necessary. I'd much rather stay in bed than get up and walk three miles, but I keep taking those steps for my heart. What better reason do you need?

I'm somebody who's had my share of allergies, and for many years I didn't understand why I had this problem. It turns out that it all boils down to the medical fact that these symptoms take over when the body's on overload and our systems lock up.

When our physical selves are under too much strain, they don't fully absorb vitamins and minerals. We go into shock, and it's almost as if the circulation slows down, similar to a blocked river. We aren't getting oxygen to our cells, and when this happens, the body goes haywire.

Now, let's say that you're allergic to corn, but strangely enough, there are times when you can eat it without any trouble. One day you get a call from the principal saying that your child has beaten up another kid in school and you must come get him. You're on your way, but the car stalls every few blocks. Then, you're remembering the fight that you had with your husband the night before over something that was probably very dumb. You wonder, *What good is it to be right if I don't win?*

You finally pick up your son, talk to your husband, call a mechanic to look at the car, and then sit down and grab a bowl of corn chowder for dinner. Suddenly, you feel as if you're passing out—and it's not just from the corn. It's from the overload to your system, which has to process both the problematic vegetable *and* a huge helping of stress.

A few days later, however, you find out that your child acted in self-defense, and you're the most wonderful parent in the history of the world because he's leading the class in good grades. You must be doing everything right! Meanwhile, you get a call saying that your bank made a mistake on your account and they're giving you free checks as a present, plus a new toaster for your troubles. In the midst of all this joy, your husband sends a dozen roses to say that he was sorry about that silly little spat. Now, eat that same bowl of chowder, and I bet that it won't bother you at all. I'm not advocating that people try out their allergies, especially if they're acute. However, know that stress exacerbates minor and moderate allergies. Don't even think of toying with an acute or severe allergy.

LIFE'S INJUSTICES

In this life, it's important that we don't enable dishonesty. You have to demand honesty from everyone—especially yourself. In fact, I've fired agents and lawyers for telling me half-truths; you better tell it to me straight, or your backside is gonna be on the highway. Tell me the bad news, but make sure it's accurate, because I won't accept anything less.

That doesn't mean that you have the right to use "truth" as a weapon or slice it up into shades of partial honesty. These practices cause most of us a great deal of undue stress, which is quite unfortunate. But standing your ground often makes the stress go away, because justice has a funny way of putting a big smile on your face.

For instance, don't go thinking that a bank can't make a mistake, because we all know that things don't always add up! One day I got my bank statement, and it was several thousand dollars short. Four words went through my brain: *Where is my money?!*

The next day, I walked into the business manager's office and told him, "The bank made a mistake with my account."

The man laughed at me and said, "Diane, the bank doesn't make mistakes."

I said, "Excuse me, but I'm a country girl from Mississippi, and I was taught to add when I was little. These numbers do *not* add up, so somebody did something wrong. You better check it."

The manager rolled his eyes and got out his sharpest pencil. Well, guess what? This particular institution was doing something illegal with the checks. Basically, four clerks were taking money out of someone's accounts—such as mine—and putting it into a master account prior to stealing it. Yours truly started the fur flying on this one and demanded justice.

I won't say the name of the bank, but at the time it was in all of the newspapers in California. I brought it all about with just four little words: "Where is my money?" I simply asked that over and over again. Country girls want answers, and you should, too—it's just that plain and simple.

I guess those clerks thought that I'd never miss the money because they were under the misconception that movie stars light cigars with hundred-dollar bills. "It ain't true, McGee," as my mother would say.

The fact is that most plumbers and teachers earn more money than the majority of actors who pay their taxes off the top and then shell out money to five other people: 1) an agent who got them the job, 2) a manager who called the agent, 3) a business manager to handle the money, 4) a lawyer who makes sure the contract is right so that they get paid, and 5) a press agent to publicize them so that people know they're working and they'll get the next job.

I'm not playing the saddest song for myself on the tiniest violin in the world. I love to work, but I can't tolerate it when a bank steals the money that I worked so hard to earn! Even worse is when someone doesn't believe me when I say that it's been stolen.

Life's injustices cause us to spiral, and there are, as we all know, so many injustices in this world. For me, personally, one of the worst is that there are 120,000 actors in the union called the Screen Actors Guild, and most of us aren't working! The reason is that it's so expensive to film movies in the good ol' USA. This means that all the jobs are going to other countries: the UK, the Czech Republic, South Africa, China, Germany, and Spain, among other places.

Our neighbor Canada, a land with great subsidies and tax incentives, has more movie productions than they can handle—but it only has about 8,000 actors in its actors' union. Cab drivers I've talked with have been pulled off the streets of Toronto and Vancouver to be in productions, because there are roles that need to be filled. It's devastating for American actors who know the sad statistics: Last year, 87,000 actors made less than $10,000—that's not even a poverty wage.

It's worse when you consider that out of that group, 32,000 didn't even make one dime acting last year. So when you read the movie magazines, know that most actors don't make $20 million a picture. Checks that size go to less than 20 human beings, who are all promoted by big-business agencies into the megabucks dream! The rest of the great artists struggle.

It's wrong to judge someone's circumstances just because they carry with them the label of actor or doctor or lawyer. You don't know another human being's situation until they tell you about it, so reserve the right to be surprised. For example, my entire life has involved dealing with hardships and the stress that comes with the struggle for a dream and the fight for survival, just like almost everyone else.

When my little girl Laura was in elementary school, she went to a private institution called the Buckley School in California. I worked really hard as a single parent to make sure that she got a great education. Remember that I'm the girl who went to a tiny school in Mississippi where if you asked for music lessons, the teacher would look at you as if you were brain-dead. That same teacher could have pointed to a piano in the corner of the room . . . but sadly, there wasn't one! Laura had a very high IQ, and she deserved the best, which is why I wanted her to get better than I got.

I remember one time when I was thrilled to be returning home from a movie set to spend time with Laura. I learned some interesting news as I was preparing to leave: My child had been all over the evening news throughout California. Laura, who was ten and in the fifth grade, had been marching outside of that fantastic Buckley School in an effort to get her poor teachers, who saw little money from the high tuition, a raise. Before I could even get home, my mother called me to say that Laura was in trouble, so I called the principal, who was what you might call a tad judgmental.

"Miss Ladd, we know you did it!" the principal accused me in a very loud, stern tone that would have made me pee in my pants if I'd been a youngster. I was blamed because they thought: like mother, like daughter. I've never run from justice and neither do any of those in my gene pool.

I replied with a laugh, "I don't even know exactly what she's done! Don't blame the parent who's on a movie set. But whatever it is that she's done, she's my little girl, so you better treat her kindly."

I dropped my briefcase in the hallway the night I got home, hugged Laura, and together we flipped on the evening news. There was my little girl leading a march in front of the school with a big sign demanding more money for her teacher.

Meanwhile, the faculty loved her. They called me and said, "Miss Ladd, your child was born to help this world!"

I'm laughing while remembering how Laura had a sign that read: "Truck drivers make more than teachers. It isn't fair!" What I didn't know at first is that two of her instructors had actually left the children they loved teaching to become truck drivers with cross-country routes. It was the only way that they could earn enough money to pay their monthly bills. These were great educators being denied the profession that God called them to do.

That night at dinner, Laura explained it all to me. "This is terrible, Mother," she said. "My teachers can't even take care of their own children."

I passed the potatoes, and said, "Honey, tell me what happened."

My ten-year-old put down her fork and replied, "Mother, you told me that we must help each other in this world. And you told me that you can't just lie down and close your eyes while letting the worst of the world pass you by."

Guilty, guilty, guilty! I told her all of the above many, many times over.

Laura went on, "Mother, you also told me that I have to stand up for what's right in this world. And you told me that if somebody is being unfair, and I can help in any way or speak up, then I should. And I did!"

"Uh-huh," I said.

"The reporters just happened to come," Laura explained. "I didn't know what was going on. I was just standing outside my class with a sign because I was very unhappy that my teacher was leaving to become a truck driver. I wanted my teacher back, and all I did was hold a sign that said, "Please don't let my teacher go.'"

I could only say one thing: "I've never been more proud of you, honey," I replied.

By the way, I ignored some administrative threats to suspend my child. If they'd harmed her because she practiced free speech, I would have been on them like a duck on a June bug—in other words, I would have gone bonkers!

I have to tell you one more school story about injustice. The next year, Laura wrote a fabulous book report on the play *Inherit the Wind*. My daughter's new teacher leaned politically toward extreme conservatism, and Laura received a D minus for her report. I was livid because, if I do say so myself, it was a great book report that was a little advanced for a sixth grader, so I went down to that school at lunch and found the teacher.

"Heeeeyyy!" I called out to her, and she stopped in her tracks. She knew that we were going to have a little scuffle about this book report, so she tried to cut me off at the pass.

"Miss Ladd," she huffed, "I just want you to know that your daughter Laura has interpreted this play in the wrong way, and it's just not acceptable. That's why I was forced to give her a D minus."

Always a good listener, which is important in this life, I let her have her say, and then when she was finished, I had a little news to pass on to this wonderfully conservative teacher. First, I began with a little honey, which is important when you're spiraling through conflict.

"I know you're so busy and have so many kids in your classes; I understand that there are many pressures. But I want you to know that I'm acquainted with the writers of a play called *Inherit the Wind,* and they're actually friends of mine," I said. "Close friends."

The teacher gulped.

"I have to confess to you that I showed these writers my daughter's book report, and they said, 'This is fantastic!' In fact, they wrote a little note to you. Darlin', let me read it out loud. It begins with them saying, 'We're just so thrilled that you inspired your students to read plays like *Inherit the Wind.* In fact, we'd love to come down and talk to your class about it.'"

The teacher began to smile and then gasped, "Oh, oh, oh! That would be fabulous!"

And she changed Laura's grade from a D minus to an A minus. She wouldn't give her an A or an A plus, which is what I thought that she deserved as a totally impartial mother (mm-hmm), but there was still that little minus, and it bothered my child.

"Leave it alone, Laura, leave it alone," I begged. "Be grateful for what you got."

The moral of this story is that I used honey to get to the teacher instead of bursting into that school and hurling out a load of vulgarities or accusations. I used sweetness—and the fact that the men who wrote this play said that Laura understood it better than most people they'd ever come across.

By the way, I never told the playwrights that Laura got a bad grade, and I never asked them to write to that teacher. I simply said, "My 11-year-old chose your play." They were flabbergasted, and when they looked at her report, they went out of their gourds. Without my even asking, they put the solution into my hands. I had the ammunition to fight my battle, but I tried to use it wisely.

JUDGMENT AND FORGIVENESS

Try not to judge others too quickly, and please don't look upon yourself too harshly. The whole world is in a state of shock over this. We've gotten faster paced, but unfortunately we haven't necessarily been brought closer together, and what alienates us is our judgments.

Part of the problem is that we receive shocking information on a daily basis, usually from a newscaster with a smile on his or her face. We hear that 15 more Americans were killed in Iraq, and it's hard not to make snap judgments as to who's at fault. We don't even have time to think about the facts because the stories about the soldiers dying are quickly followed by updates on the latest diet craze, the weather, and sports. We make up our minds without thinking about it, and then our senses are bombarded and blasted before we have the time to clear our heads, think for a minute, and perhaps reevaluate the situation.

Some of our judgments are on a smaller, more personal level. What about that new couple who just moved in down the block? You might think, *Oh, they drive a Mercedes, so they're rich and uppity. I bet their children are spoiled. Look at her strutting down the driveway, and how he's too busy to say hello to anyone on the block.*

You've made all these assessments based solely upon the type of car that your new neighbors are driving. It's a biased, unfair, and untrue way to live. It's also dangerous, because thoughts have energy that's either positive or negative. It's no wonder why so many people are overweight in this country, since weight is a buffer zone against negativity.

Make too many judgments and suddenly you'll find yourself in a unpleasant spiral. You might begin feeling physically ill and wonder why. It certainly could have something to do with all of the negativity in your life. It's a proven fact that anger releases free radicals into your system, and as I've said before, they're linked with disease and depression.

Do a little experiment for me: For just one day, try to push any judgmental or negative thoughts out of your brain. If you feel them coming to you, take a deep breath, stop, and try to think of something more pleasant. At the end of the day, take stock of how you're doing in the physical sense. My guess is that you'll actually feel better and healthier.

Judgment is a very dangerous thing, and it's really about control. Well, we don't like other people to impose their will on us. And when you judge, you're expecting something from another person; in many ways, you're playing God with them. Do you enjoy it when this is done to you?

Of course, many of us pass the harshest judgments on ourselves. I'll never forget my first real play: I was 16 years old and had joined the touring company of an award-winning play called *Tobacco Road* starring the great Shakespearean actor John Carradine, the father of actors David and Keith Carradine.

Mr. Carradine's co-star, an actress named Georgia Simmons, was visiting friends in New Orleans and saw me perform at the Gallery Circle Theater. I was invited to come to California and audition for the role of Pearl in *Tobacco Road* because they needed someone to replace a young actress from New Jersey who was leaving the show to marry a boy in Mississippi. Of course, that's my home state, so I took this as a great sign of destinies running together.

The final audition was between one other actress and me. I had only a few moments to show the character Pearl and her inherited natural grace to Mr. Carradine, and I had to do so in a walk across the stage. The first time I tried it, he stopped me and said, "Diane, you're moving like a mudslinger!"

Okay, he wanted to see a highfalutin strut, and I gave him just what I thought he needed.

"Now you're walking like some model," he complained.

But the third time I moved across the stage, he shouted, "Perfect!"

Meanwhile, the other actress who was vying for the role heard all of these shenanigans going on, which were simple acting moments. She stood up to audition and absolutely panicked, believing that she couldn't do it. She was passing judgment on herself!

It followed that her body reacted in accordance with the bad vibrations it was receiving from her mind. She wouldn't allow herself to embody the role for fear that she wouldn't pass muster. In the end, I was the one on the pay phone screaming, "Ma! I got the job!"

The point of my tale isn't just to entertain you with some theater stories, although I know that can be fun. I want to pass on the message that when we're afraid in life, it's actually possible to draw to us the thing that we fear the most.

My own father was the last man in the world who should have thought of himself as a loser. He saved thousands of animals and helped poor farmers balance their livestock. He was a man who knew how to sing and laugh, and he inspired his child to believe in herself. Ironically, right before he died, he told me that he felt like a loser because he believed that he'd been called to be a preacher but hadn't followed his soul. Perhaps this was true, but did he have to pass such a harsh judgment on himself?

None of us should think of ourselves as failures while we're participating in the great dance of life. Who are we to judge? The only person we know who walked on water was Jesus Christ, and that was more than 2,000 years ago!

I don't know about the rest of you, but I've only managed to step over a few mud puddles and that's about it. The good news is that we're all getting there. For those of you who are spiraling at this moment in time, I consider you winners because you're people who care and who want to know more, which is why you're reading this book. You're searchers, and that makes you victorious.

There's a saying I love that truly applies here: "God isn't finished with me yet." The minute you put this book down, you might get angry, use a cuss word, eat too much, smoke a cigarette, or have an extra drink. Stop passing harsh judgments on yourself, because I still consider you to be someone on the way up. God doesn't make junk, and that includes people. Your caring makes you a winner spiraling through your evolution.

Even as a child, I noticed that human beings have a way of blocking evolution. I'll never forget what I witnessed as a youngster traveling throughout the South with my father. When I was five, I saw these grown men who were heavily clothed in gray-and-white-striped shirts, trousers, and caps. They were working extremely hard in the noon sun, bent over lifting rocks that seemed way too heavy. Sweat poured off their bodies.

I noticed iron bands so tightly locked around their ankles that their flesh was bleeding. The shackles were attached to thick chains, which in turn were connected to monstrously heavy, large, black-metal balls that were being pulled along behind each one of them. They were also chained to one another. There were other men in uniforms, guarding those who were working; and they had whips, guns, and vicious dogs with them.

In a confused voice, I asked my father, "What are those men doing?"

He replied, "Well, they're guarding those other men who are very bad. They're criminals. They've done something wrong, and they're being trained to become better human beings."

Even more confused now, I asked, "But Daddy, how do you teach someone to become a human being when you're treating them worse than a dirty dog?"

My Daddy did what we in show biz call a "double take" and murmured in a low voice, "I don't know, honey. I just don't know."

Letting Yourself and Others Off the Hook

You can't evolve if you're stuck blaming yourself for things that happened in the past, which is called an "anchor." If you hold on to an anchor, it's often because you fear letting it go. If there's something you did that was wrong and that you blame yourself for, then look at it, face it, and move on. If you have to make amends, then do so, but get on with it while you have this opportunity called life.

If you don't go forward, then you'll stay stuck. Instead, just call a good friend and say, "Ohhhh, I was so wrong, and I really messed up. I was so stupid and off base. How could I?" And then talk it over with your pal and let it go. Fix it, solve it, and get over it.

The flip side of this scenario is blame, which is an ugly thing. It makes you lame, and if you're just limping along, then you're not really being. If we have an opportunity to blame someone else for our failures, then we often will. It's a human trait—and it's also wrong. A good friend is someone who says, "Hey, you really messed up, but I love you anyway. If you can, try not to do it again. Let's see what we can do about this."

I have a crazy idea: Why don't we stop judging each other's religions for starters. Our God is their God, no matter what color skin somebody has, no matter what somebody's pocketbook or bank account says, and no matter what nation they lay their head down in at night. To judge someone else fairly, you need to use your brain and some *raison d'être* . . . and you also need your heart to really feel with compassion in order to see another person with purity.

PART III

Miracles

AN UNLIKELY MESSENGER

Through a strange phenomenon, I received some unexpected and valuable information. Stick with me here. One night, Laura, my secretary Sandy, and I were watching *The Tonight Show* with Johnny Carson. Johnny's wife was a guest, and she was entertaining the audiences with stories about a dog psychic she'd visited who'd really helped one of her pooches. At the time, Laura and I were having trouble with our keeshond puppy named Christmas, who was unruly and disobedient—in other words, he was wilder than a mad hatter.

My secretary told me, "Go see that dog psychic that Mrs. Carson raved about on TV."

"Give me the number—I'll do it," I answered.

So I drove to a trailer park in the boondocks of California to meet a tiny man who knew nothing about me. At the time, we had two cars, including a new one that I used for interviews, meetings, and appearances, and a good "save-the-gas" older car. It's not as if we were living the life of Riley, no sir. I was having trouble making payments on the little house that I'd bought for Laura and me, so I worked hard at making each dollar last a long time. On the day that I went to visit the pet psychic, I used the "save-on-gas" car. Meanwhile, Christmas was in the backseat acting goofier than usual and jumping around like a loon.

The minute I saw this little psychic man, he put his hands on his hips and said, "You also have a beautiful new car that's gray." My silence told him everything that he needed to know about being right, and the fact that our crazy canine started to run in circles just confirmed it.

"Well, this lovely little dog loves to ride in that new car," said the pet psychic. "In fact, your dog loves to ride in the backseat and look at the other dogs on the street. He says to them, 'Hey, you SOBs, I'm up here riding and you're down there walking!'"

I laughed and figured that this would certainly be a lively conversation with someone who seemed to be as nutty as my furry friend. At the very least, I'd return home with one heck of a good story to tell Laura and Sandy.

"Your dog has a big ego," the pet psychic continued.

"You mean to tell me that some dogs have bigger heads than others?" I asked.

"They certainly do," he answered. "I also want you to know that this dog really loves you. And by the way, he tells me that your daughter is about to have a problem with her back."

Boom! The earth stood still, and I stopped breathing. The fun and games were over, and my smile quickly faded.

"If you don't get your little girl's problem looked at right away, it could become really serious," the man cautioned.

"Now listen," I said, "I'm a woman who lost a child. Don't you think I have my daughter's health constantly checked?"

"Your doctors have overlooked something big; it happens. I don't want to alarm you, but you must check it out," he said with a look of grave concern.

Quickly, I put my ego-ridden, mad-as-a-hatter dog in the backseat of the car that was beneath his pedigree and sped home. The next day I took Laura to see Dr. Jack Mosheim, a renowned orthopedic surgeon in Beverly Hills, and said, "Listen, I think there's something wrong with Laura's back . . . but maybe it's just my imagination." I certainly couldn't tell him that this had anything to do with a dog psychic. "I want you to check this out—check and recheck," I told the doctor, who promptly scheduled my 12-year-old for a back x-ray.

He had a sick, horrified look on his face when he came back with the results. Laura's back was curving like an "S"; we just hadn't seen any apparent changes in the way she walked or moved. My baby had a disease known as curvature of the spine, or scoliosis. Left untreated, it can cripple a human being or even kill her.

At those moments in life, any mother would find herself asking "Why?" Often, we don't get many answers, but I received a few that day when I pored over my daughter's medical history. At the age of five, Laura was at her father's house and was bitten by a black widow spider. This required a breathless trip to the emergency room and a shot of adrenaline for her.

From the studies I've done on healing and the human body, I know that this spider bite caused a sort of inner concussion, which threw off her yin and yang. It also wreaked havoc with the oily substance on each side of her spine, which is called the kundalini energy. One side began to grow stronger than the other, so it began to curve. By the age of 12, her back was slowing forming an "S" shape.

"How could you miss this?" I asked her pediatrician, who'd been her doctor since she was a baby, and he felt terrible about the oversight.

"My God, Diane, we never saw any sign of scoliosis. But now Dr. Mosheim says we must act immediately, and there's only one solution. We have to put Laura in a back brace," said the pediatrician.

"For how long?" I asked, dreading the answer.

"Four or five years," he replied. "She needs to be immobilized from her hips to her neck."

A moment that seemed like a lifetime passed as my brain began to register what this meant for my only child. "You mean to tell me, doctor, that my precious, blue-eyed, blonde-haired child is going to spend her entire teenage years from the age of 12 to 16 or 17 in a back brace?" I demanded.

"It has to be done, or she'll be crippled," said the doctor with empathy, but there was also grave concern in his voice.

My mind raced for any solution, miracle, or wisp of a prayer that might make all of the above not true anymore. *Breathe.* I knew that I needed a moment to just breathe in and out before reacting (which is good advice in any situation). My mind began to clear from the chaos, and plans were already formulating inside my head. First, I needed a timetable from the doctor.

"How long until you absolutely must put the brace on?" I asked with tears in my eyes.

"Maximum? Nine months from now and not a day later—I mean it, Diane," he warned me.

Had life not already burned me by the tragic death of my child, I most probably would've just listened to the doctor and done exactly what he wanted me to do on that very day. I would have explained the situation to Laura and set the appointment to put her body in that brace. But they say that some problems in life are actually gifts in a strange package. You just have to take the time to unwrap them slowly.

If I hadn't been to hell and back, I might have answered, "Okay, doctor, whatever you say," but that didn't happen.

The Aura Reader

I had nine months to find a miracle, and the first step was my finding this man who was an aura reader. I don't know how I discovered him or who told me about him, but there I was standing in front of this incredible human being named Cash Bateman.

Cash (nicknamed C.C.), a special person, was one of the most respected dream analysts in our country. As a little boy, he had a dream that his little dog Tippy had fallen down a well. When he woke up, his pet was indeed missing, so C.C. ran outside and checked the well. Inside, he found a shivering, crying, happy-to-see-him canine.

When C.C. was 12 and living in Virginia Beach, he had a dream that he was at the water's edge with magnificent flowers that looked like lilies. He picked one and put the gorgeous white bud to his ear, where he heard the most incredible music. The same day, he woke up, went to the beach, and found the exact flower from his dream. He put it to his ear and nothing happened—nothing. He thought he was losing his mind, since this was the first time in his whole life that one of his dreams hadn't come true.

The young boy sat down on the beach and began to cry. A man came walking by, stopped, and sat down beside him. "What's the matter, son? You dream a lot, do you?" he asked.

The shocked C.C. shared his story.

"Well," the man began and then smiled as he explained, "dreams are on three levels. In yours, the flowers represent human beings, and the music represents the music of life inside each of them. It's your job in life to help the human beings 'hear' their music."

This man was renowned prophet Edgar Cayce, and C.C. became his protégé. (He also became a war hero: At the age of 18, he was a member of Pappy Boyington's Black Sheep Squadron.)

I didn't know C.C., but a friend told me that there was a man who could read auras and who actually worked with doctors. I was desperate for any help at all, and I knew that we must search in life—it's a path. I thought that he might be a kook, but I was willing to find out.

Cut to our first meeting in his office: C.C. took one look at me and asked, "Who's the child in your aura who's on the Other Side?" He then told me the exact age my first daughter would have been if she'd lived. After this, he gazed at me with great compassion and said, "Diane, you mustn't hold your first child down. You have to let her soul go on."

I replied, "I don't hold her down. I don't pray to her or keep her here. I've already let my child go to God! In fact, Bette Davis once gave me that advice, and I told her the same thing: I'm not keeping her here. So don't you tell me I am!"

Dear reader, I must tell you something before we go on. I don't care how spiritual you are, but when someone you love passes away—anyone—there's a ripping of a cord deep inside of you. When a mother loses a child, there's such a tearing of that umbilical cord that the hurt is in your cells as long as you live. The wound remains alive in your bones. When Laura and I lost her grandmother recently, we'd talk about her, and then suddenly one or both of us would be sobbing. It happens to everyone, and that's just the way life is. But back to my precious Laura . . .

I was suddenly very angry at C.C. for saying that I hadn't released my first child's soul. "I came to you to get a reading," I said, suppressing my anger and focusing again on the task at hand. I wanted him to give me a personal session to see if he was worth his salt.

C.C. calmly looked at me on that day and said, "Diane,

let me ask you a personal question. Why did you get married a second time?"

What he couldn't know was that I had been married from 1973 to 1976 to a gentleman I'm still friendly with to this day. I call it a "three-minute marriage" because it seemed to be over as quick as it started.

My eyes went wide, and then I answered him. "Well, we were both on the rebound. We both had kids, and we were lonely and frightened. We said 'I love you' and needed to believe it. It was a mistake," I said quietly, "but we're still friends."

He replied, "You and Bruce had a destiny pattern that meant that you'd have children with him. It was karma."

It was funny that C.C. mentioned that, because little did he know that I was Bruce's second wife and that he'd desperately tried to have children in his first marriage. They'd tried everything and were finally told by doctors that Bruce was sterile. But he wasn't—I promise you! C.C. was right again and was giving me an incredible reading.

"Your second husband was just meant to be a friend. You weren't supposed to marry him," he told me.

My God, I got married to the wrong person! I should have never done it, and that's why my daughter has scoliosis, I thought. Why oh why do we always blame ourselves, when it's not close to being our fault? Unfortunately, we're very quick to play the blame game. I managed to quiet down my negative inner feelings and listened to C.C., who said many other things that he couldn't possibly have known in any conventional way. He simply read my aura.

Later, he explained that he also worked with many chiropractors and cranial therapists. He'd watch during the treatment, and by reading the patient's aura, C.C. could tell the doctor if the problem had been balanced or not. I hope medical science will someday embrace ideas that they don't even want to talk about now. Can you even imagine how "woo-woo" people thought this was in the early '70s?

By the way, C.C. worked with top AMA doctors, who made him take a vow of silence so that they didn't get in trouble. Can you imagine being "in trouble" for healing someone by any means possible?

C.C. was often admonished for his gift. His own mama was afraid of him and dragged him to church as a little boy of five and a half, screaming in his tiny face, "The preacher will know what to do with you!"

He thought, *A friend of God. Oh boy—someone will understand!*

But when the preacher walked out onto the stage, the child saw one of the darkest and most negative auras he'd ever witnessed emanating from a person. The man was yelling, "And the devil will claim you!" He even pointed his finger at the parishioners. C.C. never went to church again.

The next step was taking Laura in for a reading. My darling child sat down in front of this amazing, gifted truth seeker, and the first words out of his mouth confirmed my deepest fears: "What was the poison that entered her body when she was five years old?" he asked.

"I knew it! It was because I married someone I shouldn't have," I finally blurted out.

"Stop it, Diane," C.C. muttered. "I'm not talking about a person. I mean an actual poison."

Laura remembered that hot summer day when she was bitten by the black widow spider at her father's house and the subsequent trip to the hospital. The doctors had given her an antibody shot and sent her home in great pain.

C.C. nodded, and then asked if there were any other physical symptoms that appeared right after the spider-bite poison entered her system.

At the time, I had just gotten married to William Shea, Jr., and Laura and I had moved to New York City. One day we woke up and her left eye had crossed; at the time, I didn't connect the eye problem with the spider bite. I used some folk medicine to help, including potato peelings applied to her closed eye. To do this, you peel a potato, and at night, you place the peelings on the eye. I also put peanut oil on the bottoms of her feet. Both processes were old Southern remedies to withdraw poisons. We also went to the eye doctor, who gave Laura horn-rim glasses.

Laura would also fall and stumble more than was normal, too. I thought she might have a brain tumor, but the doctor just passed off my concerns as the rantings of an overprotective mother. It turns out that we were both wrong. What was happening was that my daughter's body energy was suffering from an imbalance caused by the poison.

Eventually, the eye uncrossed and the stumbling stopped. Who knew that there was still damage lurking inside my child, and that it was attacking her spine?

C.C. Bateman was only the first stop, since he had a lot of tricks up his sleeve. He immediately sent me to a Dr. Harold I. Magoun who was in New Mexico. He was the editor of *Osteopathy in the Cranial Field* and had also acted as one of President Eisenhower's private physicians. We're not talking about a "chopped-liver" doctor here, but an incredible mind and an amazing talent. I'd like everyone to know that these types of people are out there; you just need to be a searcher and find them, but beware of the phonies.

Dr. Magoun was one of the granddaddies of osteopathy in the cranial field. He gave Laura a treatment, and in the process sat me down and worked on me, too. This means balancing the entire body by accupressure on the skull and through the roof of the mouth. Everything is connected in the body.

Dr. Magoun felt that Laura needed her treatment to be done closer to where we lived, so he picked up the telephone and made a call to someone he knew could help. I was told that Dr. Viola Frymann was an incredible miracle lady, and I was in need of someone with miracles in her bag of tricks. Before he let me go, however, Dr. Magoun had one last suggestion.

"Diane, there's one exercise that could really help Laura. She needs to swim all the time and as much as possible. It will help with the curve in her spine," he said.

I nodded, but immediately the concerns of a single mother living on the fumes of her checkbook took hold. Despite what you read in all the movie magazines, I wasn't one of those actresses living on an estate with an Olympic-sized pool and cabana boys running around bringing me mint tea. I'd bought a home in the San Fernando Valley, and no sooner had I signed the papers than show business went into a slump. In fact, the movie business as a whole had gone to hell in a handbasket. At my tiny house, which was mortgaged to the hilt, the only water in the backyard came from the hose I used to water my flowers; I certainly couldn't water my daughter to get her better. Houston, we had another problem! I didn't have the money for a pool either (but I'll get back to all that in a minute).

Meanwhile, I traveled to La Jolla, California, to meet with Dr. Viola Frymann. She now runs a busy practice at her life-saving Osteopathic Center for Children in San Diego, treating children from many states and diverse countries, from Russia to Japan, Canada to Australia. Of course, I did a little bit of research on Viola before going to see her for the first time, and I learned that she made many miracle cures happen.

Years later, I'd taken my neighbors' children, twins with cerebral palsy, to Viola. At the time the twins were born, there'd been a nurses' strike at the hospital where their mother went into early labor. Doctors gave her oxygen, but one twin got too much and the other didn't get enough. The first child's eyes were crossed and his feet were turned in. He was five when I met him and was a fantastic little soul. The little girl who didn't get enough oxygen looked like Brigitte Bardot, but the beautiful child was branded a "basket case" with the mentality of a three-month-old, although she was chronologically also five years old. She could barely hold her head up.

Viola took one look at the little girl, and the first thing she told the adults in the room was in the form of a warning: "Be careful what you say—this child knows everything you're telling each other. Don't you think for one minute that she doesn't hear and understand you. She understands every word you're saying. In that body is a mind that knows but cannot communicate."

When the doctor was done with her work, that same "hopeless" child could hold her head up and feed herself with a fork, and she also helped the little boy a great deal. The point of my story is that even in the bleakest of times, you can't ever lose hope, because God puts assistance out there for you to find.

This was Viola Frymann, although I didn't know the extent of her powers at the time I was going through my crisis with Laura. I *did* know that she'd been a medical doctor in England, and that she came to America, got married, and had a baby. Her child died, but she knew that if the doctors had done more or known more, the infant could have been saved. This tragedy spurred her on to devote her entire life to helping children. She was a medical graduate of the University of London before coming to the United States to study osteopathy. She is a practicing osteopathic physician specializing in the problems of children. She became part of my miracle team.

I'll never forget the first day I met Viola. I sat in her waiting room talking to a beautiful young redheaded woman whose handsome husband sat beside her. "This is our third visit, and it's our daughter's last hope. We've been everywhere," she told me. "We've been to Scripps, Menninger Clinic, Mayo, UCLA, you name it."

Their three-year-old daughter had been injured during delivery when she was horrifyingly dropped by one of the nurses in the delivery room. As a result, she was retarded, and her motor mechanism had been hurt beyond repair. She couldn't walk, bend her knees, or control the use of her legs.

These parents knew that their daughter would be permanently handicapped, but their hope was that somehow she could be helped to walk. In fact, they were obsessed with the idea that this child must stand on her own two feet and walk for herself. More than once, both of them had the exact same dream where they were both killed in a car crash, and suddenly, they were on the Other Side looking at life and their child.

In their dream, their daughter had been taken to an institution, and they were watching; then one night, the building burned down. People were running everywhere, right past their little girl, who couldn't walk. She was sitting in a wheelchair crying for help, but went ignored.

The parents were looking down from heaven and couldn't help their treasure, who summoned up all of her strength and threw herself onto the ground. The child was screaming and crying as she tried to crawl across the floor with her arms to reach safety, but she wasn't fast enough and wept loudly when the flames entered the room.

At that point, they'd wake up from this nightmare in a pool of their own sweat, with a severe case of the chills. This dream came again and again, and it was always exactly the same. Knowing that they had to take matters into their own hands, they found Dr. Frymann.

Laura and I sat there stunned as we listened to their unbelievably painful saga. The man put his arms around his wife and tried to comfort her as she told us about their fears. Suddenly, the door to the inner office opened and I saw a frail-looking, 5'2" lady with twinkling eyes approach us. I assumed this must be Dr. Frymann.

She was holding a little girl in front of her by the hands and wrists. Without hesitation, as the woman lifted the child's arms, the girl bent her knee, lifted her leg, and stepped toward her parents. Another step and yet another one followed, until the beaming child had walked to the woman sitting next to us. I don't think I've ever seen an expression on anyone's face like the one I witnessed at that moment. It was seeing the smile of God on a human countenance. The universe really is connected.

There was no turning back, and I put my darling treasure in the hands of this amazing healer. For nine months, I drove Laura down to La Jolla twice a month to see Viola, who documented her progress with an in-depth series of spinal x-rays, which indeed showed some progress.

Whenever we went to see the good doc, Laura and I would have to spend the night in a hotel room, because Viola didn't want my baby to sit straight up in a car for hours after her treatments. She wanted the treatment to "take" and for her body to settle down before the long, often-bumpy car ride home. Any jostling of her spine could erase the good that had been done in Viola's office.

Speaking of which, the stress was overwhelming for me because I had to pay for a hotel, food at a restaurant, gas, and the treatment. All of this was money that I didn't really have, so I went to Bruce and asked him for some help, which just about killed me, but I did it.

He didn't seem to understand. "Diane, you're just being woo-woo. Just take her to a regular doctor," he told me, rolling his eyes.

Knowing that I couldn't preach to someone who refused to be converted, I lowered the playing field to something he'd understand. "I'm also asking this other favor for your daughter. I really need you to put in a pool at my house," I begged. Now, my ex is a good guy, and he was never really late with a child-support payment. But clearly he didn't think that his former wife needed a beautiful new pool in her backyard, so I pulled out the big guns.

"Bruce, you're starring in movies. I only took alimony from you for one short year! Your daughter desperately needs a pool for her back therapy," I explained. "Couldn't you do this one thing for us?"

His sensibilities were clouded with all of the mixed-up love and anger he had toward our relationship, because in spite of everything, he'd really wanted our marriage to work.

"You told me because I didn't hit you up for alimony that I could come to you if I ever needed anything," I reminded him.

His reply was succinct: "I'm not puttin' in a pool for you, Diane. Your friends will come over and swim in it," he said.

This was total ego on his part. He couldn't handle the failure of our marriage, so he wouldn't deal with me or any of my concerns, which is actually heartbreaking when you think about it. So many people do that in this world. But I couldn't waste my time staging endless debates with him over the topic. The nine months I had before Laura spent her entire teen years in a body cast were slipping away from me at a rapid pace.

Hat in hand, I went down to the bank to ask for a second mortgage on my house. Back then in California, they even called what I wanted a "pool loan." I got the money but couldn't build the pool right away, although I had some guys come over to break ground. The medical bills for Laura were so overwhelming at this point that I had to use the new funds to pay off some of the doctors' fees.

A friend actually made me laugh when he heard my plight and said, "Diane, I heard of borrowing from Peter to pay Paul. But I've never heard of borrowing from pool to pay Peter." You must never, ever lose your sense of humor, even when you think it's three towns over in a ditch. When you're a single parent, you do what you have to do.

Bruce would call with helpful suggestions. "Diane, if she needs to swim, why don't you take her to the YMCA," he offered. Unfortunately, the Y was a long way away, and if I was working (which I needed to do to keep paying the bills), it was hard to figure out how to take Laura for her daily swim. I didn't want others to drive her because I'd lost a child due to drowning. If I couldn't be there with her, I didn't want my girl in the water—period. Suffice it to say, I made myself available, no matter what, almost every day for nine months as we drove to that YMCA while the workers were s-l-o-w-l-y finishing our pool.

Meanwhile, we continued to work with Dr. Frymann. One day at a Thrifty drugstore in Beverly Hills, I ran into actor Ray Bolger, who played the Scarecrow in *The Wizard of Oz*. Ray had an amazing sense of joy, and once he saw me, he began to dance in the aisles of that store. I could have sold tickets because it was such a treat to see him twist like a piece of string in the air.

"How do you move like that?" I asked in an amazed voice. He wasn't exactly a young man, and I knew he'd suffered from back problems in the past.

"You go to Dr. Terwiloger," Ray sang to me as he danced. "That's who! Go to Dr. Ter-wil-oger!" He did a few high kicks right in the cough-syrup aisle, then stopped moving for two seconds to tell me that Carol Channing hurt her back on Broadway, and she'd flown in this great Dr. Terwiloger to help her; Jonathan Winters would come over from England for a treatment.

As I researched this lead, I heard rumors that Dr. Terwiloger, who lived in the Valley, would only charge you a tiny bit of money for each visit. A true genius has a way of not bilking his clients.

Soon, Laura was one of his patients, and her team was complete. We had Dr. Viola Frymann, who performed osteopathy in the cranial field; Dr. Terwiloger, who worked to balance her body with chiropractic adjustments; healer Doug Johnson; and guardian angel C.C. Bateman to keep tabs on Laura's aura—and the rest of the crew. I was so grateful that my guardian angels were getting to all the right people that my fear faded. I knew that these individuals were givers and not takers; I was in the right company.

Laura was the trouper of all troupers and never complained, even when Viola worked on her. "Did it hurt, honey?" I'd ask her when we were back in the hotel that night.

"It hurt some, Mom," Laura would say, "but she's helping me."

My young daughter was this gentle, willowy creature with the courage of a lion. This was the same little girl who, the first time she had a small role in a movie, *Foxes,* went to school skipping, believing that the other kids would finally think she was so cool. But instead of saying "Congratulations," her classmates just taunted her.

I told her, "Jealousy is a sad thing." And then I read her my favorite poem by Thomas Wolfe, which begins: "Pity is a learned emotion. Children know it least of all."

During those nine months, Laura didn't take any pity on herself, but threw herself into her swimming and treatments, while I watched the calendar with dread. Those weeks were over in the blink of an eye, and then it was time to go back to our original family doctor and an orthopedic specialist named Dr. Jack Mosheim of Beverly Hills.

There were 20 people in Dr. Mosheim's office on the day we went to see him, and he happened to walk past and see Laura in the waiting room. "My God!" he yelled. "Diane, growth is the worst detriment when it comes to scoliosis. And from the looks of it, Laura has grown about two inches since I saw her last time."

My jaw dropped, and everyone in the waiting room began to stare at me like I was the worst mother in the entire world.

"We have to get her in the back brace right now!" the doctor practically screamed.

Shame mixed with guilt filled my entire being. Here I was, Miss Woo-woo. Had I allowed my child's condition to worsen?

"First, we'll take an x-ray to see how much harm has been done in the last nine months," he said in a stern voice. "You'll have to listen to me and put the brace on the minute I get the results." I could see Laura fighting back tears, and I grabbed her hand. I'm not sure if I was giving her comfort or seeking some for myself.

An hour later, Dr. Mosheim came running back into the lobby waving the x-rays in the air. In front of those 20 other people, he screamed words I'll never forget: "My God, it's a miracle!"

I just looked at him and said the same thing that I did the day that Laura was born. "You're right, doctor. It's a miracle . . . and a helluva lot of hard work," I murmured.

"Come into my office immediately. Nurse, hold all my calls," he said, ushering Laura and me into his private office. The minute we sat down, he reached into a desk drawer and produced a handheld tape recorder, which he clicked into the "on" mode. "I want to know everything you've done," he said. "I'm going to go before the medical board and tell all. Your child's spine is almost perfectly straight."

I mentioned Dr. Frymann, the osteopath; and the chiropractor, Dr. Terwiloger. Dr. Mosheim, an orthopedic surgeon, didn't smile. His profession is still in an ego battle with osteopaths for supremacy. Comedy and tragedy know how to work together onstage to produce beautiful results, but most doctors still aren't smart enough to figure out the whole "working together" thing.

The minute I mentioned the healer, his eyes fell to the floor, and when I got to the aura reader, he turned off the tape recorder! My daughter's spine was almost a straight road with no curves, but that doctor never told any medical board. He wasn't going to have his peers look at him and say, "An aura reader. 'Lucy, you got some 'splainin' to do!'"

Not everyone can be a Joan of Arc and spread the word. I tried to get the news out myself, but I didn't have the venue in those days. At night, I thought about all the other children going through their teenage years in back braces who might have been helped by just hearing Laura's story. I was proud of my daughter and me, but sad for the rest of the people out there who were being denied the chance to benefit from having an open mind.

I'll give you a little footnote. Some 20 years later, my elderly mother Mary's back went out. I took her to the same orthopedic surgeon, Dr. Mosheim. He did some good for her, but I couldn't help thinking, *Oh, doctor, if you'd followed the path of truth—not that of least resistance—what you might know today.*

Opportunities for growth in life can quickly pass us by, so we need to reach out and grab them when we get the chance. It's a small universe with a big picture, child. You just have to look beyond the first few glances for the real answers.

CHAPTER 10

VERY SPECIAL MOMENTS

When Laura was doing the film *Mask,* Barbra Streisand stopped by the set one day and asked director Peter Bogdanovich, "My God, where did you find a blind girl who could act?"

Peter answered, "She's not blind. That's Diane Ladd and Bruce Dern's daughter."

Barbra said, "I thought that child was blind! I thought she'd never seen anybody in her life. She must be wearing special contact lenses."

Peter shook his head. "She's not wearing anything on her eyes, Barbra," he replied.

What Miss Streisand didn't know is that Laura and I had gone to a stable run by Liz Lukather, an amazing woman, partially paralyzed by polio since childhood. She became a doctor, even though no one wanted to let her into medical school. She owned a riding stable for disabled children and taught those kids how to ride horses.

Laura went there to learn how to ride as if she couldn't see, because she had to do so in this movie. Liz put a blindfold over my daughter's eyes and taught her how to feel the horse and then how to sense any fence or other object that was invading her space.

While I was there, Liz showed me a child who'd been in a drowning accident and then had been revived. By the time he was conscious again, his oxygen had been cut off long enough to cause severe brain damage. He had a look on his face that seemed to indicate that he wasn't cognizant of his surroundings.

I couldn't help but think of my first little girl, who'd hit her head in the pool. Instead of feeling grief, however, I just watched Liz put these special children on horses. Their entire faces changed—only by fractions, but you could see that something was different. They knew that on a horse, they could do something; they had control of that animal. It was one of the more astonishing experiences of my life.

I've seen a similar phenomenon while working with disabled children for the Special Olympics. It was amazing, for lack of a better word. Standing alongside the professional athletic volunteers, including Rafer Johnson, we'd watch these young potential athletes in their precompetition minutes standing by the side of the gym. For example, we'd observe a child with cerebral palsy wait on the sidelines with his shoulders slumped. But when the music blared over the loudspeakers and it was time for him to do his number and be "on," it was as if he knew that it was his moment in history to fulfill his destiny. My God! The shoulders would come back up, the body would change, and the child would move forward to do a tumble, beginning his award-winning performance.

I've watched these moments with tears in my eyes. They also make me think about how our society has changed for the better. Two hundred years ago, these same children would have been pushed off a cliff to get rid of them; they would have been tossed away and deemed worthless. This is a good lesson for all of us. You don't judge a book by its cover, and you don't judge the soul in someone else's body. The impossible dream *can* be possible.

For example, my friend Christopher Reeve was one of the most gorgeous men who ever walked across a room. He wound up totally paralyzed, debilitated, and breathing with a machine, and look what he accomplished with those barriers as a new starting point for him. Chris didn't commit suicide; instead, he went through the pain and started an organization to help others. He influenced millions of human beings and helped just as many through his own suffering with his unflagging courage, along with his amazing heart. He gave by example, which proves to me that there's so much good in this world.

There are other special angels who have touched my life. Years ago, Princess Diana invited Laura and me to England because *Rambling Rose* was her favorite movie. She hosted a gala reception for us at the palace. Prince Charles was too busy to attend, so Diana came alone.

Laura and I were in the receiving line when the princess approached us. Standing inches in front of me, the beautiful lady took her long, white opera gloves off to shake my hand. When Princess Diana shook your hand, she looked you right in the eye; her soul looked right into your soul. This was one of the most incredible women I've ever had the privilege to meet. She was a glorious being.

A Very Special Night

In 1992, Laura and I were both nominated for Academy Awards for *Rambling Rose*. We were completely over the moon! It was the first time in the Academy's history that a mother and daughter had been nominated in the same year.

That was just the beginning of an amazing ride. For a long time, it seemed obvious that my daughter and I would also be presenters at the Oscars—but then we were told that we wouldn't be. It was just more of the politics that dog this industry. There were certain people's nieces who were in an obscure TV show that were presenting instead, and there were a lot of games being played, which is the "same old, same old" in Hollywood.

All the women's organizations were livid, God bless them. Women In Film called Gil Cates, the producer of the Oscars, and said, "How dare you not have the first mother and daughter nominated in the history of films also presenting? We want to see these ladies together on the stage!"

What a hoot! I knew from my other studies that whenever there's positive energy being combined from all sides, negativity doesn't have a shot in hell. Laura and I suddenly represented mothers and daughters everywhere, and I knew in my blood that we'd be presenting. That was confirmed when my agent called one day and said, "Diane, I don't think the Academy is too happy about this, but they've been forced to make you and Laura presenters."

Our date that night would be my beautiful mother, so we'd have three generations of Lanier women combining their positive energy on that momentous occasion . . . but there were a few more stumbling blocks before we got to the big night. For starters, at Oscar time you need to have one humdinger of a dress and borrowed jewelry for the ceremony. There are people who also lend you dresses, often asking for them back in the morning so that they can sell them.

But sometimes no one lends you anything, and you have to go out and buy a gown that could start at $10,000. I was enjoying my acclaim, but I was at another point in my career where I couldn't afford to drop that much cash on an outfit.

Enter designer Mary McFadden, one of the classiest acts in all of fashion. She called me and asked if she could design my dress for free, and I could have wept for joy. (Meanwhile, Armani called Laura with an offer, which wasn't small potatoes either.)

McFadden not only made me the most magnificent Oscar dress, but she also made my mother something beautiful to wear, too. She even gave me four other outfits for that time period, because I'd be required to attend many events. Suddenly, the woman who was once more worried about the mortgage payments was wearing $50,000 worth of evening gowns; one of my jackets alone cost $12,000. I wore those clothes proudly for Mary McFadden.

On Oscar night when I walked out with Laura to present one of those little golden statues, the entire Academy was cheering us. Of course, all of those people sitting in the audience clapping had no idea what it really meant. None of them were privy to my personal life—they didn't know that I'd lost a child and almost died of a tubular pregnancy, or that top doctors had told me that I'd never have another baby. And there was my daughter standing straight and tall at the Academy Awards; that was better than any prize.

The sad truth in Hollywood is that you can't win if the people who are releasing your movie only put up $75,000 to promote your Oscar campaign while the studios running against you are spending $2 million. Money talks! That's called an unbalanced race, but Hollywood is never really a fair place. No one said it would always be just, but we still kicked a little dirt.

I didn't come home with gold, only golden memories. But I'm sure that one day Laura and I will be nominated again, and we'll be thanking God, the Academy, and a slew of other people who made it all possible when it seemed to be impossible.

CHAPTER 11

THE EFFECT OF HELPING OTHERS

Susan Strasberg, one of the greatest actresses on this planet, starred on Broadway in *The Diary of Anne Frank*. Of course, her father was the amazing Lee Strasberg, one of the leaders of the famed Actor's Studio, which is the most prestigious acting group in America.

When Susan was starring on Broadway, she bought a house on Fire Island and gave it to her parents as a present. When her mother died, her father had the house. The point is that Susan was a very generous human being; when she did have money, she gave to all in need. Then came the show-business slump in the late '90s and the absence of roles for women who were over 40. Here was one of the greatest actresses who ever lived, and she didn't even have health insurance because she couldn't pay the premiums.

Susan was diagnosed with cancer, and in addition to the horror of hearing such devastating news, she was overcome by her inability to pay for medical treatments, and she felt shame about how her life had turned out. Her famous last name prevented her from letting the Screen Actors Guild or Actors' Fund know that she was down and out. Often they can help in extreme cases, but Susan was a Strasberg, which meant that she suffered in silence.

At the time, the City of Hope hospital in California had named me "Woman of the Year." Now awards are lovely, but there are other types of honors in life that are much better. Picking up a phone and calling the hospital board of directors about Susan gave me great pleasure. The biggest win of all was when they agreed to treat her cancer free of charge. Unfortunately, Susan didn't take the gift and go to that hospital for fear that people would find out. Instead, she made an additional medical appointment with a healer in San Francisco. She believed in this man and actually moved to the Bay Area so he could see her.

Over the next two years, we weren't in the same city and only communicated by phone. She told me that she was getting better, but other friends who actually saw her on a more regular basis said that she was very swollen in the stomach. They thought that this healer person was ripping her off. (Remember that although I believe in healers, they must be good ones. You need to keep an open mind but be skeptical at the same time; and I personally was devastated that Susan hadn't accepted some help and generosity from that hospital.)

Right before Susan died, a friend took her to the emergency room at a very well-known hospital in New York City. After they did some tests, they told her that her illness was serious and that she should go back to the man who'd been treating her! She was too ill to travel anywhere, but her friend told me that the hospital emergency doctor and nurses put a coat on her and gave them both the bum's rush. She was obviously dying, but she received no treatment because she was broke.

This was the same hospital that had a Lee Strasberg wing! I was told that the family had donated a million dollars to the hospital, and now Lee's daughter was turned away when she needed medical help. This was a total abomination and a tragedy. Why not put her in the hospital that night and have a gentle death?

The next morning, Susan told a friend on the phone that she felt very cold and was lying down to rest. She was also waiting at home because she'd called a man to come over and buy Marilyn Monroe's pearls from her. Marilyn, who was like a sister to her, had given her this lovely necklace, which was one of her prized possessions. Susan finally knew that she must sell them in order to get the money for medical treatment. She died that morning, It's a strange mystery as to the destiny of the pearls.

When I got married on Valentine's Day 1999 to my husband, Robert Charles (more on him in a minute), Susan was going to be one of my matrons of honor. Her dress was being made, and she said to me, "I'm truly better, Diane. Your wedding will be my coming-out party." She was going to fly to California for the ceremony, but she died five days beforehand.

On my actual wedding day, I let the man who was supposed to be her escort that day walk down the aisle alone, and I kept her name in the program. It said "Matron of Honor, Susan Strasberg. Great lady. Great friend. Great actress. Great humanitarian. She will be remembered in death as she was in life." I'd also had special compacts made for my matrons of honor; I gave Susan's to her daughter, Jennifer, who spent a little quiet time with me after the wedding.

"Honey," I told her, "if you ever feel despondent, look in the mirror in that compact. Gaze into your own eyes and see your mother . . . and know that you're never alone."

I want to take a minute here and talk about free radicals and cancer. I know many people who have been cured of this disease, but they've done much more than go through chemotherapy (although chemo has been known to save lives).

Some of my friends who recovered chose not to undergo this conventional form of treatment, but instead used alternative modalities, but some friends did employ it. Many who depended strictly on chemo and traditional American pharmaceutical medicines—for example, my friend Joan Shawley, once dubbed "one of the greatest comedians that ever came from this country"; and my friend, writer/director Jane Cusumano—chose chemo and died. The process kills the cancer cells, but also destroys many good cells in the body.

There was the famous case of Jim and Donna Navarro's four-year-old son, Thomas, who was diagnosed with brain cancer, known as medulloblastomo. I was able to speak to Mr. Navarro personally about his wishes for his little boy. This family refused to give the little boy chemotherapy treatments for his cancer, and our courts intervened and threatened prison if they wouldn't allow the chemo. The Navarros begged for the right to have Houston, Texas's Dr. S. R. Burzynski's anti-neoplaston therapy treatments. These treatments had shown great results against medulloblastoma with few side effects! So much time was wasted while they were forced to wait. The horror of this case, in the opinion of Mr. Navarro, is that too much chemo caused hemorrhaging in his little son's young, depleted body. The loss of this child remains a great tragedy.

There are some facilities in this country that seem to have more choices available in healing modalities when it comes to cancer. I'd like to know why the Food and Drug Administration (FDA) and AMA aren't working with those places and sponsoring their research. Why is so much money given to pharmaceutical companies who invent drugs that have side effects such as heart attacks and strokes? Pretty scary, isn't it? It seems to be a big corporate money game with profit and loss being the bottom line. "First do no harm" should be the guiding principle of all doctors, companies, and other individuals connected with well-being.

My daughter, Laura Dern, is very frustrated and angry. She has waited to give her son, now four, his preventive-care inoculations until this year of 2006, because she was informed that the pharmaceutical companies would finally be removing mercury as a preservative. It had been suggested that these preservatives could cause harmful results such as autism! When we were all inoculated as children, the antibodies were alive . . . then the pharmaceutical companies discovered how to save *money* by adding chemicals such as mercury to act as longtime preservatives! In spite of all the fury vented by parents, the ban on these preservatives has been lifted for probably another two more years until 2008! I guess, then, that the leftover excess will just be sifted over to developing countries. Aren't the children of the world's lives, and our future generations, worth more than money? What's going on here?

Daniel Haley, a New York legislator, has written an amazing book called *Politics in Healing,* and, although I certainly don't know all the answers, I do also admire a statement made by former Iowa Congressman Berkley Bedell, founder of the National Foundation for Alternative Medicine. He wrote: "The universe has given us a cure for everything, although it's up to us as human beings to find those cures." I wish Susan were still alive to find her cure. I miss her.

What Can You Do?

Many people say, "But I have a job and the kids. I don't have time to help anyone else on the planet, although I'd love to be that kind of compassionately engaged person." I have a suggestion: Why not pick just one thing and invest your time and resources in it? Fight for your local school, better medicine, or the rights of abused children or the elderly. You have the time to take on just one cause, so stop saying that you can't and just pick your battle and do a little bit to help. This is the only way we'll clean up everything in this messy world. Remember that if you don't have time to help, nobody is going to have time to help you, so let's join together and change the world!

I'll tell you one more story while we're on this topic that shows how our feelings and attitudes can affect our physical and mental well-being. Olympia Dukakis (a Greek-American actress), Ellen Burstyn (an Irish-American actress), and yours truly (a shiksa from the South) were playing Jewish ladies for the film *The Cemetery Club,* so we went to a Hebrew center in Pittsburgh to do some research.

Once there, we met up with a charming elderly lady named Sarah, who was the hostess that day, and she showed us around. At the same time, she was helping make some Russian immigrants, who'd just arrived in the United States, feel at home. In the midst of the busy day, they brought out a birthday cake and sang to our lovely hostess.

"My goodness, how old are you, Sarah, if you don't mind me asking?" Olympia inquired.

"Well, I'm 102 today," she replied.

"What?! It's not possible! Sarah, my goodness, what vitamins are you taking?!" I cried. The three of us couldn't believe it.

"Well, you know, Diane," she began, and then laughed. "When I was in my mid-80s, I started to feel ancient and sorry for myself because my body was getting old on me. Finally, I looked in the mirror, shook my finger at myself, and said, 'Sarah, you stop thinking about yourself all the time. Try to do something for somebody else while there's a breath left in you.'

"So I came down here and volunteered one day a week. Then it became two days, and then three," she continued. "Now I'm here five days a week. My home is about one mile away. People used to drive me, but then I started walking, unless it's too hot or too cold. And at 102, I feel ten times younger than I did 20 years ago."

This woman is an example for all of us.

CHAPTER 12

MY WOO-WOO STORY

Okay, here's the big woo-woo story—are you ready? I'm going to tell you a tale that will blow your mind, and it begins with great sadness. . . .

When my first child died, it was almost the holiday season. I'll never forget that Christmas because it was a horrible, lonely time for Bruce and me. People didn't want to be around us because they didn't know how to act or what to do or say—and we didn't either. With no family nearby, we were all alone in our mutual depression.

One day we got a call from a man named Ted Lala (yes, that was his real name) who said that he knew us. He was having a holiday party for about ten people, and he invited us to come to his home for Christmas dinner. Ted promised us, "You'll have a wonderful time. I've invited a woman who starred in a Broadway show, another actor, and a composer. You and Bruce are both so talented, and I promise you an amazing dinner and a quiet holiday celebration. We're going to have songs, and we'll sing; you'll enjoy yourselves."

This man was a total stranger to me, but I thought that he knew Bruce. In turn, my husband figured that he knew me. Later on, neither of us could even figure out how he got our home phone number, because we'd never met Ted Lala in our whole lives. But I said yes to his kind offer because we had no other invitations.

On Christmas Day, we went to Ted's house and it was, in a word, *wonderful.* For those few hours, I forgot my pain because he threw a joyous celebration to mark the birth of Jesus. His guest list combined people of both the Jewish and Christian faiths, but we didn't talk about religion. It was a day of love, and I soaked it all in, thinking how immensely grateful I was to him. At his house, I smiled for the first time since losing my baby.

A few days later, I sent Ted a thank-you note but got no response. Later, I tried to call him, but could never reach him (these were the days before everybody had an answering service). The number he gave me was never busy either; it just rang and rang.

I didn't see Ted Lala again, and there were times when I thought back to that Christmas and decided that maybe the man didn't exist at all. Perhaps he truly was a guardian angel who was placed here to give two grieving parents a moment of relief.

Some 12 years passed, and it was 1976. I won the British Academy Award that year, and there was a lot of publicity swirling around me during that time. I also had a movie near release, *Embryo,* with terrific actor and friend Rock Hudson. Also, even making me much happier than that film was an offer I'd received to *star* in a terrific play on Broadway.

I was extremely busy. The phone was ringing off the hook. One night I heard another call coming in and decided that I had time to squeeze in one more conversation that day . . . and it was Ted Lala on the other end! My jaw dropped because it seemed that he really did exist.

"I'm having another dinner party, Diane," Ted said breezily, as if 12 years hadn't passed with absolutely no contact since that Christmas get-together. "It's very important to me for you to come to my dinner party, and I'm only living five blocks away from you now, so it really should be no inconvenience."

I felt so indebted to Ted for helping me when I lost my child that I didn't hesitate. "You got it," I said.

He continued, "There's a man who saw your picture in a recent magazine, and he mentioned to me that he knows you from a past life and wants to talk to you about it. He'll also be at the dinner. Will you agree to talk to him for me?"

"I will definitely talk to this man, but first could you answer a question, Ted?" I asked him. "How did we meet in the first place?"

"Oh my, Diane!" he exclaimed. "I have someone at my door. See you at the party."

A few days later, I found myself driving the short distance to Ted's new home. I found him in his kitchen cooking, and as promised, there was another man sitting quietly by himself in the living room. This person was huge to the point of being about 200 pounds overweight. In fact, he looked like the Roman emperor Nero. Ted brought me into the living room, introduced us, and then left us alone. Looking around, I noticed that there were no other guests.

Once our host had left, I started talking about the coliseum in Rome for no reason at all. The man got a very strange look on his face and blurted out, "Have you ever been to Italy, Miss Ladd? Have you ever walked around the coliseum?"

I nodded, because I had indeed been to that magnificent place.

The man continued to speak: "I have to talk to you, and I know you're going to think I'm crazy. But I saw you on TV acting in a show, and a whole past life flashed in front of me . . . and I knew it included you." He went on to tell me that an extremely long time ago he really was Nero and had many, many wives.

"You were my youngest wife. You were 15 years old when your father gave me your hand in marriage," he told me. "I thought you were still a virgin, and I never slept with you. You were my pride and joy."

Sitting down slowly, I continued to listen to his story. He told me about his beloved general, a great war hero, who kept his kingdom safe from war. When there was a threat, he sent out this specific general because he was brave, strong, and won all of the battles.

"One day someone told me you were having an affair with my general," he said. "You were in love with this man behind my back!"

Suddenly, a cold chill ran down my spine.

"And I put you to death because of it," he said with great remorse coming over his wide face. "I did it in such a way so that people didn't know. I had you die during a sport in the Coliseum. I tied you to a post and let the bulls tear you with their horns."

"Ahhhhh!" I cried in horror.

"I put a mask over you so that no one knew who you were, because you were very beloved by the people," he said. With a look of great anguish on his face, he continued. "I'm so sorry, and I've come here tonight to ask for your forgiveness."

What does one say after hearing this type of a story? Actually, I had one question: "What did you do to the general?" I asked.

"Oh, I disgraced him. I made sure that he lost his next battle, even though it cost me a territory," he said. "We lost many soldiers—brave, strong young men—in order for me to get my revenge. It was a shameful act on so many levels. I took away your life and his power."

At that point, I lost my appetite, so I excused myself for a moment to go find Ted in the kitchen. Strangely, he was nowhere to be found, and the food he was cooking was gone. There was nothing to do but leave the house. The man walked me to my car and said, "I'll probably never see you again, but I want you to verbally tell me that you forgive me."

Although it was a lot to absorb, and I hadn't had time to process the information, I wanted to let this tormented soul off the hook. "I'll forgive you," I said, "but on one condition: Don't you ever do anything like that again! Either in this life-time or the next!"

He nodded, and tears filled his eyes.

"Now you're forgiven," I told him.

I never told a living soul this story because it was just too strange and much too woo-woo.

Several years later I met a lovely doctor from Florida, and we became engaged for the next six years. I dearly loved him, and he was a great physician, but I never felt that it was actually the right time for us to marry. Ladies and gentlemen, always pay attention to those little nagging feelings.

While we were together, however, there was great love between us. We had a lot in common, too, including a belief in past lives. One hot sunny day in Florida, we began to have an in-depth discussion.

I asked, "Are there any past lives you feel are unre-solved?"

My gentle fiancé looked at me with great sorrow and replied, "There was one lifetime where I felt very betrayed. I had a love, but she was very young. It was in Italy, and I was a general in a great army. I loved this girl, but she was the youngest wife of Nero. I loved her so desperately, and I thought she loved me.

"But then I lost battles, and I was disgraced. When I came home, she'd never see me. I couldn't find her, and she wouldn't talk to me because I was a failure. She only loved me when I was a success, but not when I lost," he said with great pain.

Wide-eyed, I yelled, "That was me! And what were you doing sleeping with a 15-year-old girl and the wife of a king? You put me in danger and then left me unprotected—the king killed me!" I told him the rest of the story, and the lifetime he remembered was exactly parallel to the tale that man told me in Ted Lala's house.

True or false, credible or crazy—I can't tell you. Is this woo-woo time or something that really happened? Either way, it's a heck of a script, in my opinion. I want to see a network miniseries based on the story I just told you. It still blows my mind because it's a huge spiral. I knew this doctor in a past life, and I recognized him again in this one.

But my tale isn't over. Another person who liked to talk about past lives—or in his opinion, the cellular memory of consciousness retained and passed on in the DNA—was my dear friend Marlon Brando. In one of the first conversations I ever had with him, I said, "If I told you what all the psychics say about us, it would scare you to death, Marlon."

"Nothing scares me," he replied, "except the fear that I might have a child fall into a body of water and hit her head."

For a minute, I almost stopped breathing as his words floated through the air, and that wasn't the only thing he said to me that struck some ancient nerve. I always had reasons to believe that I knew Marlon in the past, based on so many things that mostly must remain private between the two of us. What I can reveal is that I believe we have the opportunity to catch up on a lot of things in each lifetime.

By the way, I never saw or heard from Ted Lala ever again. When I went to his house a few months after meeting Nero, Ted had moved, with no forwarding address. Do you think he still knows where I live?

PART IV

Fate, Love, and the Future

FATE

About ten years ago, I was dating an extremely successful man in the aeronautical industry who was charming,
divorced, and fervent in proclaiming his great love for me. He
had a gorgeous home in Bel Air and spent hours on the phone
telling me how he was going to marry me . . . uh-huh.

During that time in my life, I began hemorrhaging during
my period because I was short on progesterone. The doctors
gave me another hormone test but didn't check my progesterone. I had three D and Cs (dilation and curettage) before they
figured it out, and they only did so because I conducted my
own research and suggested that this might be the problem.

Landing in the hospital for a final D and C, I was weak and
tired from all the hoopla. But this man I was dating cheered
me up because he brought me flowers when he visited. And
on Saturday night when I came home, he arrived around din-
nertime with ice cream and then tucked me into bed early so
that I could rest. He was very sweet.

On Sunday morning, I got up to go sit in the sun. But then
the voice of intuition spoke up, and I asked myself, *Diane, do
you think this man is being faithful? He has another woman in his
house with him right now!* You must always listen to your little
voice.

Charging around my home, I was stopped by Laura, who said, "Mother, stop running. Why are you moving so fast when the doctor said you have to take it easy?"

"I'm going out, Laura," I answered, searching for my purse and car keys with reckless abandon.

"You're not supposed to drive. The doctor said you've got to rest," she lectured me.

"I'm going over to my boyfriend's house. My little voice just told me that he's over there with another woman!" I ranted. "I'm going to go catch him and get the truth right now."

"Oh my God, mother! You can't go alone—and I'm driving," Laura replied.

She took me to his beautiful home on Sunday morning at 11 A.M. I knocked on the door, and the man who professed great love for me answered in his robe. He didn't move from the doorway, but he had a friendly smile on his face and appeared to be glad to see me, so I forced a grin of my own.

"Hey! I was just passin' by," I said. "My daughter is taking me for a ride to the beach, and we decided to pay you a visit."

"Great!" he replied and leaned forward to give me a tiny hug.

He was still lodging his body against the doorjamb when suddenly I shoved that big ol' oak door open wide and stepped into the house. I guess I forgot to wait for his invitation to come inside! Making my way toward the living room, I tried to be casual until I noticed something—or rather, some*one*—out of the corner of my eye. And that someone was looking at me through a crack in the bedroom door!

It was a brunette in motorcycle garb peeking out. I won't name names, but she was a society gal who was all dressed up like a biker babe for a morning of bedroom fun. I don't know what those two were doing with each other or what they were playing, but it wasn't good. By the way, her peeking out the door was for a reason: She wanted to be seen.

"Oh, honey," rambled my boyfriend in a casual voice, "that's my decorator."

"What exactly is she decorating?" I demanded. I'd had enough, so I turned toward the door.

He quickly moved in front of me to block my exit, while screaming on the top of his lungs, "I love you! You can't leave me! I love you more than any woman I've ever loved in my life!"

"Wow! What a crummy script—what bad dialogue," I snapped at him.

Laura came flying out of the car. Oh, sweet Jesus! She was screaming, "I can't believe you hurt my mother!"

Ignoring her, he asked me, "Aren't you going with me to Paris to the air show? We'll have a wonderful time!"

I looked at him and in the calmest voice said, "Honey, I'm at a show of hot air right now." And then I got in the car.

"I love you so much, and I want to marry you someday!" I heard him scream as we pulled down his driveway, and later on, he sent a messenger with a love letter and flowers. Then he came over and pounded on my door, yelling, "We can't let our love walk away!"

"We don't have any love," I retorted. "Our love is a sham." He could take his hot buttered rum and . . . give it to his decorator, Miss Harley-Davidson.

A few days after the breakup, I got a call asking me to lecture on health issues. Knowing that it would feel good to do something for other people, I decided to go to San Diego for the event that weekend, although I really felt like locking the door of my house and never coming out.

I arrived at the American Holistic Medical Association meeting only to find that more stress was being heaped on my plate: My name had been left out of the program, which meant that no one knew I was going to lecture, and no one would show up. In other words, I'd made the trip for nothing—I'd be lecturing to empty seats and the white walls.

That was one of those little life moments that make you want to scream. It was one week after my last D and C, and I'd just caught a man who'd said he loved me with a mystery bimbo. I was there to save the world, but no one was coming to be saved! As human beings, we do get these tests, and let me tell you one thing: I was a sad little test case.

The powers in charge of this event figured out that I was pretty upset. There was a Dr. Gladys McGarey who was in charge, and she went to another doctor on the board who was supposed to be their peacemaker. She told him, "You've got to come and help apologize to this actress who's lecturing for us, but we left her name off the program, and no one will show up to listen to her."

"What in God's name is an actress doing lecturing for us?" asked the so-called peacemaking doctor. "Plus, I can't talk to some actress because I have to attend an important lecture on cancer."

"You come with me right now and apologize to this woman," Dr. McGarey insisted.

A colleague accompanied him, and the two docs were walking down the corridor together when a woman who was attending the event stopped them. "Excuse me, I heard Diane Ladd was lecturing," she said in a breathless tone. "Where is it? When is it? I just can't miss her!"

"Who is Diane Ladd anyhow?" the peacemaker inquired, and his colleague told him that I was starring as the songwriter Belle in the *Alice* TV series and had been nominated for an

Oscar for playing Flo in the movie *Alice Doesn't Live Here Anymore.* (I didn't want to play the same character again because my sights were set on Broadway, but I later decided to try my hand at TV. I won a Golden Globe for the first six episodes of the series, and the papers wrote that I took the show from 35 to 75 million viewers.)

That first doctor said, "I never watch television; I don't have time."

His colleague laughed and replied, "Well, I always watch *Alice.*" He was one of 16 people who came to my lecture. That day I said to my small group, "They say the show must go on. I never found out who 'they' are, but everybody go ahead and move closer."

After the lecture, the friendly doctor came backstage and looked at me oddly while slowly nodding. "I've just had this incredible déjà vu. I feel as if I've known you in a past life," he said.

My body language changed immediately and became queenlike. As I stood taller, I responded, "Oh really . . . and where was that?"

He cleared his throat, embarrassed, and then continued, "At the time of Akhenaton and Tutankhamen and—"

"Aha!" I exclaimed, and to his astonishment, I rudely turned on my heel and swiftly moved away. This *actually* was a memory I knew something about. The confirmation was just too startling. I just couldn't handle it. We met later at a cocktail party and chatted for a few moments.

A year passed, and I went to El Salvador on a fact-finding mission for my country. During my trip, I picked up a strange parasite and I was one sick cookie. A slew of medical professionals couldn't figure out what was wrong with me, and I thought I was dying. Then Dr. Gladys McGarey told me, "I want you to go see that doctor I brought to your lecture."

He was a specialist, and one of his fields of expertise was parasites. Nine tests later, he found the one I had, treated it, and saved my life. He also believed in alternative modalities, so he put me on medicine, vitamins, and made me get massages. In two weeks, I was a different person.

A year later, he chaired a seminar at UCLA, and then we started dating. Eventually we were engaged, and I spent all of my free time helping him in his clinic in Florida. Yes, now you know how I met my Florida doctor! But none of this would have happened if I'd stayed home and hadn't done the lecture in San Diego after my boyfriend cheated on me. I was on a downward spiral at the time, but I knew there was nowhere to go but up.

During the next several years, I was taking healing courses, and my doctor fiancé was very much into the subject, as well as past-life regression. In fact, the government had called him about a very important political leader from another country they wanted him to treat. He felt that he shouldn't—and he didn't. This was a man who went with his gut feelings and little voices, and I admired him for it tremendously.

He was an incredible physician, and the type of man who'd jump out of bed at three in the morning with just his pajama bottoms on to go to the hospital. If you got sick, you wished to God that he were your doctor.

Once, a man's heart had stopped, and he was clinically dead. My fiancé was pounding on his chest, telling him that he must live . . . and the man listened that day and came back to life. In another instance, a man's wife had a stroke and couldn't take care of her husband any longer, so my fiancé quietly arranged for a nurse to clean up the house and make sure that the man ate three meals a day; my guy paid for it out of his own pocket.

He was a good person, and I cared for him greatly. We were engaged for six years, and during that period I spent a great deal of time working with him at his clinic, doing medical-intuitive work. I also did healings when he asked me to help. He'd take me into the hospital after 1 A.M. when the other doctors weren't around so much. I'd put on a white coat, and my fiancé would say I that was his assistant, Rose.

One time there was a preacher's wife who was going to be operated on the next morning. I went in and gently took her hand. I was trying to send energy from my eyes to hers in a subtle way without saying that it was a healing. I thought that I'd fooled her, but the minute I stepped outside the door into the silent hallway, her voice rang out loud and clear: "Thank you, Jesus!" she screamed on the top of her lungs. "She has healed me, Jesus!" We started running out of the hospital for fear of being caught.

There was another woman who'd gone into a coma after collapsing in a supermarket. She was in a deep sleep for three days, and the doctors were about to write her off as being near death, but we did our best, and she regained consciousness.

Another girl needed help, but her family didn't believe in healing and wouldn't allow me in the room. I discovered around that time that being an ordained minister ensured that anyone over the age of 18 could ask me for help, so I became a member of a church that ordained me. The process took several years, but it was so worth it.

How I Was Fated to Help Others

I have a rule that I'll never do healing while I'm acting because it really depletes my energy. Of course, there are times when we have to break our own rules because the hand of fate is tapping on our shoulder.

While filming *Rambling Rose* in Wilmington, North Carolina, there was a young actress named Lisa Jakub who played my daughter in the film. One morning I woke up at 4 o'clock, worked all day, and was just about set to go home to pass out, when I was called into a tiny production office on the set. I was told that Lisa had had a terrible accident. She was doing her school lessons on the set while sitting in a chair that had wheels on it; then she leaned back, and the chair tipped over. Lisa hit the floor with her spine, and they took her to the hospital in an ambulance.

Some members of the crew had heard about my healing work, although I'm not sure how, because I rarely spoke of it in those days. One person wanted me to call the hospital, so I did. I spoke to my young colleague's mother, Jane, who was crying and told me, "Lisa is in such pain! Please come see her."

It was midnight, and I had to be at work the next morning at 6 o'clock to do my biggest scenes. But I went to the hospital anyway, sternly reminding myself about the rule to never give a healing while I was acting.

Lisa was in agony, and my heart hurt for this little girl. I told her mother that I'd break my rule and give her a healing that would ease her suffering for the night, but that she needed to have the doctors help in the morning, because the pain would certainly return. I also asked her to not tell anyone in the acting company about what happened.

"And Jane, one more thing," I added, "they're going to tell you that it's the fifth vertebra, but it's not—it's the seventh one.

Please remember these words." After I'd eased Lisa's anguish, I went home, and the next morning I had such a lack of energy that felt as if I were getting the flu.

When I arrived on the set, a crew member said to me, "Oh, Diane, you did give Lisa a healing, and you said it was the seventh vertebra. But the doctors said it was the fifth one, so you're wrong." There's always a critic.

Months later, the movie was over, and I returned to my life. Then one day I received a call from Jane Jakub. "Diane, I just want you to know that Lisa is still in a great deal of pain," she said. "The doctors haven't helped her. And then your face flashed in front of me and I heard you saying, 'Remember, it's the seventh vertebra.' They've been treating the fifth one all this time, but I went to the doctors and told them to check out the seventh."

Can you predict the rest of the story? Jane continued, "At first they said I was crazy, and they told me to leave the doctoring to them. But the truth is they've been treating the wrong vertebra. The doctors were wrong and you were right."

Now, I'm not a white witch or anything else along that realm. I'm just a highly intuitive Southern woman. As human beings, we should all make an effort to use all of the gifts the universe has given us.

"Jane," I said, "you're her mother. You *are* there to help with the doctoring. You demand that these people do right by your daughter." I'm happy to say that Lisa made a full recovery after that conversation.

By the way, my fate was not to marry my doctor fiancé. We parted as friends, and I'll always admire his amazing healing talents. It's nice to know that he had respect for mine.

CHAPTER 14

LOVE

I'm not sure how I feel about love at first sight, but I do believe that certain relationships in your life are simply meant to be. In 1999, I found a soul mate when Texas native Robert Charles Hunter entered my life. Honey, it's a humdinger of a story.

I met Robert in one of the most spiritual spots in this country: Sedona, Arizona. A successful businessman, he was there searching for himself. He'd been divorced for two years and had already accomplished his goal of retiring at age 50. But he thought that there was more to life, and he was seeking out what could be. Forget business dealings, he wanted to deal with his soul. He'd gone to Arizona specifically to attend a course called "The Sedona Intensive," taught by a man named Albert Gaulden.

At that time, I was single, relatively happy, and content. And then one day my little voice told me to go to Sedona. Even though I had a houseful of guests coming that weekend, I gassed up the car and started to pack my bags.

Even my mother asked, "Diane, what's going on with you?"

"I don't know," I replied. "All I do know is that I'm heading to Arizona." And then I was off.

Arriving in town with my secretary, who was helping me with a writing project, I found a message waiting for me. The Sedona International Film Festival had asked me to give an award to Mary Steenburgen and Ted Danson because I'd been the recipient the year before. I'd already declined, not knowing that I'd be in town, but now that I *was* there, I told them that I'd love to do it.

Meanwhile, Albert Gaulden—astrologer, author, metaphysical teacher, and a friend I've known for years—was living just four doors down from where I was staying! Hearing that I'd arrived, he immediately came over.

"Diane! We're going to dinner Wednesday night—my treat," he said.

"No, I'm not. I'm writing," I replied. "But thank you, Albert."

He wouldn't take no for an answer. "Diane, we *are* going to dinner!" he insisted, and for some reason my little voice told me that I wasn't going to be cooking that night.

The two of us drove to Troia's Italian family restaurant that friends of mine owned. They made wonderful meatballs, but on that night the place was closed due to an electrical failure from an evening thunderstorm. Albert pulled out of the parking lot in search of another option, and I didn't see another car following him. Our next stop was the most fabulous, chichi, five-star restaurant in town, and that other vehicle pulled up right next to us.

Albert leaned out, calling to the two men in their car, "Say hello to Diane Ladd. She's the actress I told you about."

Oh God, I thought. *Who are these people?* There's nothing that I hate more than when someone invites me to dinner and brings other people who just want to meet "the actress."

"Albert, what are you doing?" I whispered with an angry sigh.

"Well, Diane, these are my two students, and I asked them to join us," he said. "Didn't I tell you?"

"You didn't tell me squat," I fumed.

"It's okay, it's okay! Isn't it okay?" Albert begged. "Please, Diane, let it be okay!"

Looking like utter hell, with a turban on my head and wearing absolutely not a speck of makeup, I walked into the restaurant feeling lower than a ladybug clomping through mud. I was wearing a slacks outfit in a color I'll call your basic ugly chopped liver.

Robert Charles Hunter was waiting at the table in this fabulous restaurant with another man, who was a doctor. Both were here on spiritual retreats to begin a deeper life journey. Meanwhile, I was pretty ticked because I don't enjoy looking like a bag lady in front of complete strangers. We were only sitting for a few minutes when Robert leaned over to me and said, "Well, what do you do?"

Albert shrieked at the top of his lungs, "He's kidding, Diane. He's kidding! I told him you're a movie star—I told him!" And then the entire restaurant was looking at us.

"Hush up, Albert," I scolded him. "This man doesn't know the difference between Diane Ladd and the man in the moon—you're embarrassing me. Besides, I'm not a movie star," I continued. "I'm an actress, which might not be good enough for you, because you like to hang out with the stars. So let's just leave it alone now." Those two men were looking at us like we were stark-raving loons!

"I told them that a movie star was joining us," Albert shot back, because he was no shrinking violet either.

"Hush up," I repeated, and inside I was mortified.

Robert had the good manners to ignore this little outburst. He glanced at me and asked, "So what do you really do?"

With that, it was his turn to get some of my fury. I glared

and said, "As long as you live, don't you ever ask an actress what she *really* does. It's rude." I was ready to slug a man I didn't even know!

At that exact moment, a young woman stopped by the table and interrupted the action by saying, "Miss Ladd, I've seen *Wild at Heart* so many times. I just loved your performance! I felt that I needed to tell you, although I'm so sorry to interrupt your dinner.'"

"Thank you, that's very kind," I told her, watching Robert's eyes go wide. It was that lightbulb moment when he thought, *Okay, maybe she really is an actress—whatever that means.* This was a man who never went to the movies—ever.

Albert had the nerve to put his two cents in at that point. "Diane, you're doing the presentation in two nights for Mary Steenburgen. I can't get a ticket, and I really want to go," he said.

At that point I knew why he'd wanted to have dinner together. "Albert, I don't know if I can get you in. I'm just presenting, for God's sake," I informed him. "It's a little late for me to ask for seats at a sold-out event."

"Try and get us three tickets," he pleaded.

"I'll try," I said, biting into a dinner roll with disgust.

At the end of the meal, Albert told me that he needed to run a few errands on the way back, but I replied, "I need to go straight home." Then Robert asked if I needed a ride. What I didn't know was that Albert was pushing us together because he'd done both of our astrological charts—without informing me, of course.

"I'll take you home," Robert repeated his offer.

To which I huffed, "I go home with the people I came with! But thank you anyway." I wish that I could describe the look I gave him, but he took it in stride.

Then the strangest thing happened the next day. I *did* get one extra ticket for this black-tie event. With a pure heart because I'd truly forgiven him, I called Albert to invite him, secretly hoping that he couldn't make it. *Maybe that cute Robert Charles from dinner could go,* I thought. Then I stopped short. *Diane, you don't even know him,* I scolded myself.

Albert called me back later that day. "Darling, I'm so upset I can't even put it into words! I can't go to that awards dinner with you because I have to give a lecture down in Phoenix," he said.

He let a beat pass. "You do know that either one of the men who are studying with me could escort you," my always-helpful pal suggested.

"I only have one ticket," I told him, hoping that it wouldn't go to the doctor.

"I think it would be wonderful if Robert would go with you," Albert said. "Do you remember him?"

"Oh, I think I do," I said, as if I didn't care. I did refuse my friend's request that his student pick me up. I informed him that my secretary would be taking me to the event, and this new man could meet me there. I didn't know him, so he sure wasn't driving me. "He can escort me around the ball. I'll meet him in the lobby," I said before hanging up.

In the ballroom of one of Sedona's most famous hotels, this 6'2", 220-pound attractive man with broad shoulders and sandy hair stood in a tuxedo, not even remembering what the actress he'd seen two nights before looked like. The woman he'd met had her hair up in a turban, wore no makeup, and was dressed in basic-blah brown.

"Could you tell me when Diane Ladd walks in the door?" he asked the event organizer.

"Oh, you'll know when Miss Ladd gets here," the official shot back with a smile.

A few minutes later, this blonde in a tastefully low-cut black evening gown, with silky long hair and the most professional makeup job in history, came walking through the door. A pack of reporters went running in my direction.

Robert said to the event organizer, "Could that be her?"

The press was running toward me, calling, "Miss Ladd! Miss Ladd!"

Robert thought to himself, *Oh, my God! Maybe she is a movie star!*

Breaking through the crowd, I noticed Robert and mentally commended myself on my good taste in men, because he looked devastatingly handsome in his tux. A few seconds later, I walked up to him and shook his hand. "How are you?" I asked. "Come on—let's go!"

For the next two hours, I was my most gracious self. It was fun to introduce Robert to other actors and actresses, directors, and camera people who'd arrived to celebrate Mary and Ted. There was a big, beautiful banquet table, but I never had time to eat because I was "on."

When it was almost over, Robert looked at me with great concern and said, "Diane, I've been watching you all night. You must be hungry. Let's get something to eat."

My secretary Liz had appeared by my side, and I told him, "Just follow us to this restaurant I know."

"Oh no! Go with Robert in his car!" Liz cried. (I didn't realize that she also thought he was cute and wanted to fix us up.) "Look, I'm going to go home, and he can even bring you back later," she said in a hopeful voice.

"Liz," I told her with stunning calmness, "we'll meet Mr. Hunter at the restaurant." I was such an idiot, but I didn't know what to do. Suddenly I felt like I was 17 years old all over again, and I wasn't sure if I should ride alone with a nice-looking boy in his car. What a hoot!

It turns out that the only place open for dinner at that late hour was the Red Planet Diner, Sedona's best greasy-hamburger joint. We got milk shakes, fried pickles, and hamburgers, and they tasted as good as a gourmet dinner. We were dripping pickle juice down our chins, and I sat in the booth in my black evening gown having a wonderful time. Robert looked pretty darn cute with mustard on his fingers.

After the burgers, we stood in the parking lot while Liz discreetly waited in my car. "Robert, it's been charming," I told him. We chatted about mindless things for the next few minutes, and he informed me that he was leaving Sedona the next day. We also talked about how he liked to write poetry, and I had to smile. A man who had a football scholarship in college wrote poetry? I learned that he was also an Aries, which meant he was the kind of man who'd be first on my list—and in my heart.

"Look, if you ever get to California, call me," I said, with an odd feeling of overwhelming regret washing over me.

"I will," he replied.

We hugged good-bye and then looked up at the sky. It was March, but suddenly it was snowing hard in those mountains. For a minute I worried about Robert because he was in a very hot-looking new Ferrari, which would be going down those icy and twisting roads. And when he pulled away, I worried about something else: I felt that I was losing my future.

Now we have to go back to the part where I was a little sad when I came to Sedona. I was never someone who'd dated much over the years. In many ways, it was heartbreaking to end my engagement to the Florida doctor at my age, because I began to question myself: *What am I doing? Who am I going to meet who's better for me than a brilliant and kind doctor?*

I spent the next six years seeing a few people, but not really getting involved with anyone special. Before my trip to

Sedona, I had a birthday, but I ain't tellin' you any numbers! Let's just say that I was still spiraling toward greater wisdom.

As my birthday had approached, I decided, *I'm not going to feel sorry for myself. I'm going to give myself a party.* Some 88 people came to my home, and it was the best shindig of my entire life so far. Michele Lee sang for everyone; and a writer, Scott Alsop, read from *Winnie-the-Pooh.* We just had a great time that night sharing our love, warmth, and talents.

The mother of one of the actors who attended the party is a top psychic. She approached me at one point and said, "I'd like to give you a reading as your birthday present."

Why not? I thought, so we moved into a quiet corner of the room, and she launched right into the specifics of what she saw on my horizon.

"Honey, you're about to meet your soul mate," she said, and I had to laugh. Frankly, I didn't believe her, but I thought it was a sweet birthday present for her to give me this lovely fantasy. Snore, snore, snore—my soul mate, sure. Tell me another good one, uh-huh.

"You'll meet him within three months—maybe sooner," she continued. "He's from the South or maybe somewhere like Texas. He's newly divorced, and I think he's an Aries. You'll form a partnership."

"What is he—a director?" I asked.

"No, he's not in your industry; he's a businessman," she replied. "And you'll marry him."

I had to be honest with her. "You have two chances of this coming true: slim and none," I told her with a shake of my head. "I married a man outside my business once, and I'll never do it again."

"You're wrong, honey," she said. "You'll marry this man. He's very affectionate, and he'll be crazy about you—he's gonna worship the ground you walk on." Then she said something that made for a sleepless night: "Diane Ladd, you haven't truly been cared for—not really. You don't even know what love is. And this man is going to love you more than you've ever been loved before."

All I can say is that it sounded so, so, so good. Bring it on!

That night when Robert pulled out of the hamburger joint's parking lot, I got into my car with Liz behind the wheel. I turned around in my seat to watch Robert drive down the street and toward the dark mountain range.

He was about a half mile in front of me, but through the lightly falling snow, I saw him stop at a red light. As his taillights turned toward the left when the light changed to green, something powerful happened to me—and I went nuts! "Oh my God, my God!" I started screaming to Liz.

"What? What's wrong, Diane?!" she asked as she drove with an extremely concerned look on her face. "What's happening?"

"Oh my God! That man is driving out of my life, and he's not supposed to leave. I've done something really stupid! I've done something foolish. What am I doing? I've done something wrong!"

"What are you talking about, Diane?" Liz asked, gripping the wheel.

"I've done something very bad!" I ranted and raved. "What am I going to do? It's all wrong, all wrong. . . ."

"Why don't you just call him up?" Liz suggested. At our most hysterical moments, it helps to have the voice of reason sitting in the bucket seat beside you.

"But I don't have his number," I wailed. Can you even imagine a grown woman like myself acting this way?

"I have his number," Liz said in a soft voice.

"What do you mean, you have it?" I demanded.

"He's staying at Albert's other condo north of town," Liz said, with a huge smile on her face.

We hurried home, and it was midnight when I put the key in the lock and then ran to the phone with my secretary a step behind. What I didn't know is that Albert told anyone who stayed at his condo to please not answer the phone because he counseled those who needed help with alcoholism. He received calls night and day from people who needed that help, and he didn't want to burden his guests.

But when the phone rang at midnight, something told Robert to pick it up. Of course, I'd made Liz place the call. "Mr. Hunter, Miss Ladd would like to speak with you," she said in her best English accent. To this day, Robert jokes with me: "I'll have my people call your people—oh wait, I *am* my people!"

Finally I got on the line and said, "Hello, Robert. We're not sleepy"—meaning Liz and me. "How would you like to come over and have a glass of wine?"

"I think that would be great," he replied.

"By the way, do you have any wine? Because we don't," I said.

"As a matter of fact, I do. I'll bring it."

He arrived at 12:30 A.M. on a very snowy night. Meanwhile, I sent Liz upstairs so that I could play Doris Day. I fixed the pillows and tended to the fire while fluffing my hair and skirt. Gorgeous music was playing in the background while my brain screamed, "Aren't you a little old to be acting out a scene from *Pillow Talk?*" I shushed myself because I was doing it no matter what.

After Robert arrived, we started talking, which led to him rubbing my feet. I'm so provincial that I kept my socks on! So I guess you could say we had *safe socks.* Listen, when people talk about how movie stars are risqué, take it with a grain of salt; that's just gossip-magazine stuff. Any woman who hasn't been dating for a while is a prude. I am, and so are most actresses I know.

Eventually the two of us went outside on that special night and beheld what I still believe was a spaceship. We saw the lights: It stood still, and then it moved—and we realized that it wasn't a star or an airplane. Then we looked at each other, and I whispered, "Oh, that's a spaceship. Let's run inside." (As if the glass could protect me.)

Finally, we said goodnight, and I hugged him. In that moment, it felt as if my whole heart opened. Then he leaned down and kissed me, but I was overwhelmed by what was happening inside me. It's sad that most human beings won't allow themselves to feel so deeply because they're afraid of being hurt, but for once I just let go and allowed myself to experience those emotions. I highly recommend that you try it.

The minute I shut the door, I returned to my regular self and thought, *Well, I'll probably never see him again.* But my heart had been knocked for a loop all the same. When I walked upstairs, I heard Liz turn over in her bed and call out, "Diane, what were you doing? Look at the time!"

When he'd arrived at half past midnight, I'd told him, "Robert, we can only talk for an hour and a half, because I have to get up at five in the morning to drive to Palm Springs."

He agreed because he had to head back to Texas before the crack of dawn. Then when he got in his car to go, he commented to himself, "Well, I'll be damned. You spend all this money on a new car and the clock doesn't work!"

Then he looked up and saw hints of the sun rising. "Certainly it couldn't be morning."

When I walked upstairs and heard Liz, I looked at the time, and it was indeed 6:30 in the morning! In absolute shock, I wondered how this was possible. Robert and I were in some kind of a time warp, thinking we'd only been together for about an hour and a half, when we'd actually been talking for five and a half hours!

Two weeks later, he came to New York where I was a guest on Sally Jessy Raphaël's talk show. We spent several wonderful days in Manhattan, including taking Robert (who isn't Catholic) to St. Patrick's Cathedral to light a candle for his mother. We went to art museums and plays and then walked to the Palm Court at the Plaza Hotel to eat caviar and drink Bellinis (champagne and peach juice) while listening to beautiful violins.

While we were there, his tie was drawing all of my attention, and it was really bothering me. "Robert, who gave you that tie?" I asked in an inquisitive voice.

"Um . . . oh, I pick out my own ties," he said, but I knew that he wasn't quite admitting everything.

"Yes, but while you pick them out, who gave that one to you?" I asked sweetly.

"Uh, why?" he replied in a nervous voice.

"Well, whoever gave it to you is coming between us right now. It's a lady, and she's angry with you at this time. She's sending us strong negative energy," I said.

"Umm . . ." he stalled, with a pensive look on his face. Nothing more was said about the subject, but as we left the hotel an hour later, I noticed that Robert wasn't right behind me. He was actually talking to a security guard.

"How would you like to change ties?" Robert asked the young man. He took one look at Robert's $150 Zegna tie and unknotted his own $10 Kmart number.

"You bet!" the guard replied.

As Robert exchanged his beautiful piece of silk for an ugly, brown synthetic, I thought, *I could really go for this guy.* We continued on to the Essex House hotel across from Central Park to have dinner, and I said to myself, *I'm falling in love with this man.*

A few days later, I invited him to Los Angeles for the premiere of *Primary Colors.* I had a huge, great part and was thrilled with the movie. Mike Nichols, who'd directed the picture, had even written me a letter saying that he knew I'd be nominated for an Oscar—and then I got the second letter in which he said, "I'm so sorry, Diane. We have to cut out 45 minutes, and you're the only one we can eliminate without ruining the movie." It broke my heart.

I portrayed a character based on Bill Clinton's mother, Virginia Kelley, opposite John Travolta's "Bubba" character, who was based on Clinton. It was easy to love the role because Virginia was a true original, and I'd had the pleasure of meeting her in Washington, D.C.

It helped my disappointment to have Robert at my side the night of the premiere, and I even joked with him. "Do me a favor," I said, "Don't ask anyone here what they do, and believe them when they say they're an actor." It was our little inside joke, referring to that night we met in Sedona.

From that moment on, we've been together almost every single day, except for two weeks when Robert took his grown children (two daughters and a son) to Mexico to scuba dive and tell them that he was in love. It was my job to call my daughter, who in turn phoned my mother, Mary.

Laura told her grandmother in a very dramatic voice, "Grandma, we're going to dinner with Robert Charles Hunter! Mother doesn't just call him Robert; she calls him *Robert Charles.* Grandma, this is big. I'm serious, we have to go check him out."

These special ladies in my life went to dinner with Robert and me and began by giving him the evil eye, but around the time that the first course arrived, my mama was charmed by him. "You're so bad, Robert Charles," she purred. It warmed my heart because at that table I saw a family.

Robert didn't propose to me. We were in New Orleans for our six-month anniversary of being together when I turned to him and said, "You know we're getting married, don't you?"

He stammered, "M-m-married?"

"Yes," I said. "Let's get engaged."

After nearly passing out, he replied, "Okay, but if we get engaged, let's not do things too quickly."

"Oh no, Robert Charles," I agreed. "Let's set the date, though."

"When would you want to have the ceremony?" he asked in his normal voice.

It was June, and I told him that I'd like to tie the knot on the following Valentine's Day. He said okay, thinking that was ages away. Ladies, even with the good ones, you need to give them a little shove. The next thing that man knew, he was walkin' down that ol' aisle!

On Valentine's Day, the processional began with my god-child Bellina Logan, who's a great actress; and Kelly Stone, Sharon Stone's sister. They were my flower "ladies," wearing the most beautiful pink dresses and tossing sweet-smelling flower petals. My little 80-year-old mother walked me down the aisle.

Before the wedding march began, Bellina whispered, "Diane, are you all right?"

"Yes," I gasped, but I couldn't get my breath.

She said, "My God, you've been up for three Oscars. What's the matter with you, Diane?"

"Bellina, that's just an Oscar. This is my life, and I'm scared to death!" I whispered back.

My sweet Robert wasn't frightened one little bit. He was sure that he was doing the right thing, and he didn't have one shake. I was confident in him, but nervous as all get-out because it was still such a big step. It helped that I had my daughter and he had his son at the altar. Laura read a poem and started to cry, which almost destroyed me.

The great actress Della Reese, who's also a minister, married us and provided a few moments of comic relief. At one point in the ceremony, she addressed the 300 attendees: "Has anybody got anything to say to stop this wedding? If not, then keep your mouth shut from now on, and stay out of their business! That's what's wrong with most marriages. Everybody wants to get into everybody's business!

"I'm not kidding you," she warned my guests. "Stay out of it! This is their marriage and their life. You just send them nothin' but good." Yeah, Della! She should preside over every set of nuptials in the world.

Everybody said that it was the best wedding ever. Robert and I wrote special vows. They were hot, baby, and I ain't telling you what I said. All I can reveal is that it inspired a lot of people to get real serious about their futures. Three of our friends got engaged within weeks of our ceremony—we definitely were sharing the love!

People said, "This wedding is great! I want one." Even a 50-year-old writer I know who'd been a bachelor his entire life decided to finally ask his girlfriend for her hand in marriage.

Love was in the air, honey. I don't want to make light of this because love is the highest part of all of us. It's the river of purity, and we shouldn't throw mud in each other's rivers. This passion doesn't hurt—it should only seek to heal.

My story proves that love knows no age. My grandmother got married for the last time at 84 years old, but I know so many ladies out there (and men, too) who think that they'll never find that special connection. I hear: "But I have such a bad track record." Well, that kind of thinking spirals you down in a bad, bad way.

If you have a tough history with love, you're not going to fix the problem until you raise up your own energy and create a better life for yourself. Only then will you attract an improved, high-quality type of person. If you think of yourself as unworthy, you'll actually get someone who's not good enough for you. Think about it for a minute, and then decide.

It's probably also best not to focus too hard on finding love. Do some spiritual work or take an exercise class. Begin by doing something to open yourself up before you move on to others. You can't just sit there and wait until you meet a member of the opposite sex, hoping that they'll "fix" you.

But that's what many of us do, isn't it? We want our mate to mend us, and they can't do it. First of all, it's not their job. You have to love yourself before you can care for another. If you don't feel the best toward yourself, how in the heck can you give that affection to another person?

Love is tricky because when you first meet, it's all "Whoooooeeee!" Then what happens next is that you acti-vate and start mirroring each other's stuff. I think that living together is kindergarten, while marriage is college; those vows ask you to grow up.

Now why does love churn up all of our own stuff? Why is intimacy so rigorous? The answer is because all of us remain in the school of human growth for our entire lives. Each friendship, each love, requires us to bring forth all that's unfinished and wounded in ourselves so that we can transform into something more magnificent. To mature, we have to learn to walk before we run.

Your soul has to learn to go through this process, too. Love takes a soul that's moseying along and revs it up to the point where the joy is mixed with vulnerability and fear. Our challenge is to reach out to others anyway.

As for matters of the heart, I believe that every human being is entitled to love, and I think the reward comes when you stop blocking it. You evolve yourself to a higher level to attract someone who has also stopped deflecting true emotion and is ready to receive, too.

One last thought: Whomever you love is never going to be 100 percent of what you want. My thought is if you get 60 percent, then you're doing great, kid. When you get more, you're just plain fortunate and lucky. And when your mate exhibits the other 40 percent that you don't like so much, then just take a deep breath. We're people—welcome to the human race.

WHY MEN AND WOMEN CAN GET ALONG

My friend John Gray wrote the "Mars and Venus" books, and he hit it right on the head—men and women are totally different creatures:

- Women like to fight; men don't.

- Women like to talk; men usually shun it.

- Women like Fluffy the cat in bed at night; men want to choke that animal, but they don't dare because then his mate would choke *him.*

I'm just kidding about the last one, although most men I know really don't want the pets (especially their hair or fur) on the pillows.

Relationships are very complicated, but not impossible to figure out if you think about your mate's past. For example, if you're a woman, it's helpful to look at your honey's environment as he was growing up. Did his mother treat him like a man, or did she embarrass him? Did his parents abuse him?

Many boys suffer this maltreatment, and that's a tragedy in this country. One out of three women have been abused, and so have one out of five men. Maybe the situation wasn't that dire for your man, but I can probably guess that he didn't get hugged enough as a child. It's likely that he grew up with parents who wanted that new car or new house more than a hug at night from their child. Isn't that pitiful? We live in a sad, sad world.

There have been several reports that marriage is actually better for men than it is for women. To have a woman in the home seems to give men something that improves their health and extends their lives. So why can't they just get along with us and we with them? The answer is simple. For starters, I've learned that men want space, and they long for this more than women do. We want to be enclosed, and they like wide-open spaces. It's just that clear-cut, and you can look to childhood habits to figure out how the sexes were never alike from the get-go. For instance, when little boys run away from home, the first thing you should do is tell the cops: "Look for a little boy with no clothes on." Very rarely do little girls strip their clothes off. Boys want their space to the point that they can't even bother with pants or a shirt!

The whole object of this battle of the sexes is that you have to fight for your own rights while keeping balance and harmony in your life. At least you have to attempt to achieve both of those things, so during a conflict, why not try to use communication instead of yelling? I think of exchanging ideas as that little "help" button on the computer. The whole idea is to heal and not hurt in life; don't be afraid to press the help button. If someone hurts you and you want to confront him or her, don't attack. The old adage of two wrongs not making a right really does apply here.

There are many gender differences during any conflict. Let's say that a woman has a problem with a contractor, doctor, or a husband. The minute the communication goes wrong, then she'll get emotional:

- "But whyyy didn't you call me?!"

- "But whyyy didn't you say I looked thin in these pants?!"

- "But whyyy was your ex-wife at the mall at the same time we were?!"

And when she gets emotional, the man in question will withdraw. Again, I don't care if it's your landscaper or your mate of 20 years. Get ready for the spiral, and it's a never-ending one. The more women get emotional, the more the men spin the other way. The solution is so simple: Ladies, detach and step back during conflict; keep your emotions in check. We usually don't do this, but it's one step at a time.

Now, I have a little confession: I'm not very good at staying emotionless during the heat of battle—although it's still good advice. I try and try and try to stay calm, but if the argument escalates, I'll eventually get to the point where I'm seeing red. I'll think, *God bless you. But now you better watch out 'cause I'm gonna jump your bones!* (And I don't mean that in a good way.)

The simple fact is that women are more emotional. When that lid comes off the pot of womanly emotion, we just explode. Let me take you behind the scenes on a movie set. Any director worth his salt will know that when an actress starts yelling, she isn't mad. Instead, she's scared.

It's the same with life: Most of us yell when we're afraid. If someone's screaming, "You rotten son of a biscuit eater!" just touch their arm and ask, "Honey, what's the matter?" I guarantee that if it's a woman doing the yelling, her anger will vanish, and she'll probably just burst into tears.

Basically, women love to talk, talk, talk forever. We love to hear ourselves yak, yak, yak. As for the men in our lives, they hate it with a capital H. They're under the impression that all that chatting means that we're attacking them. They also believe that they need to fix something, but they can't get to it because we're still jabbering. The man basically thinks, *I have to fix it right now. And if I don't fix it immediately then I'm not any good.*

Meanwhile, the woman doesn't want any of his fixing. The hell with that; we just want our men to listen to us. I don't care if you do something or not—just hear me.

I don't know if we can ever resolve this specific battle of the sexes, although we *can* be aware of what our partner is thinking and consciously try to work on it. I'm honestly hoping that another solar change might bring some answers here. Maybe they have the solution on another planet.

When I hear of worlds that have blown up over the course of time, I don't think that the reason was an unstable atmosphere or a meteor attack. I just know that it was a man and a woman on that planet arguing. One of them said, "I'm not taking it anymore." She hit a button and the whole thing blew—bingo, bango, bongo!

The flip side of this is that we all make mistakes—moi, especially. When someone brings to your attention that you've messed up or have hurt him or her, you have to stop and listen, even if it tries your sanity. You're not perfect, and there's always room for a little life improvement.

So, if someone points out a shortcoming—be it a mate, a teacher, or your co-worker—you can give them a minute of your time to figure out what hasn't been accomplished correctly.

They're not saying that you're a bad person; they're not even saying you have to fix it. You're a good person who just messed up, as we all do from time to time (except moi, of course!).

Men, Women, and Pets

Right after Robert and I got married, my housekeeper, Claudette, was feeding a stray cat that was hiding in our garage. She couldn't take the cat into her home because she already had a feline named "Tout Petit" (which means "little one" for those who don't speak French). This little one had grown into an enormous 40-pounder; he was going to remain king of the household and wasn't about to put up with any newcomers.

Winter was coming, and Claudette confessed all about the hidden feline. "It's getting cold, and I don't want her to live outside. Please—you must take in this little stray cat!" she pleaded with me in her French accent. At the time, we had three dogs, which was enough for my new husband, who insisted, "I just don't want the dogs on the bed."

He also made it clear that we'd never have a cat, because he had absolutely no use for them. This stray was an adorable black-and-white cat, so I went to Robert and asked him if we could have another boarder. He said, "I'm just not going to do it." It was his final answer, although Robert is usually very open-minded.

"Robert," I replied, "how can we not take the cat, one of God's creatures?"

"Because, Diane, I don't like cats," he said in a matter-of-fact tone.

I asked him why he didn't like cats, and he had to think about it for a few minutes. When someone tells you they hate something, just ask them why. The answer might surprise even them.

"I don't like them because they don't mind you like dogs. They won't come when you call them," he replied.

"Look, I tell you what," I challenged, "call this cat. If she comes to you, then can we keep her?"

"Then she can stay," Robert sighed, and then immediately called out, "Come here, puppy, puppy, puppy!"

I think he did the puppy thing to challenge me. Meanwhile, the stray stopped in her tracks on the porch and looked directly up at him. Then, just like Mae West, she slowly sauntered up to him, rubbed against his leg, and hopped up on the bench next to him while purring.

With a shocked look on his face, Robert, who's a very fair man, said, "Diane, we'll name this puppy Sunshine."

To this day, our "Sunshine" sits on his shoulder while he is reading his paper. It makes me laugh just to think about it, because sometimes God's creatures hear more than you think—and that includes husbands.

We also had "issues" about the dogs on the bed, and I thought, *We'll see.* In fact, when we first started dating, I had a beautiful home, which I let my mother live in while I stayed in the cute little guesthouse. I was off to do a movie, so I let my friend who was getting divorced rent my cottage.

Then the movie fell apart, and I was homeless. I moved into the house with my mother, living in the attic room, which had an old-fashioned Murphy bed. I was also dating Robert, who's a strapping 220 pounds. We spent our nights on the Murphy bed with two dogs on top of us. Of course, it was one of the best times in our lives, and we look back on it fondly. That's the way life is: Sometimes you just throw out the rules and sleep in a pack.

One more thing about men, women, and relationships: My bottom line is that you can grow together, or you can grow apart, but you *will* grow in any relationship. No one can stop the progress, so you must deal with it wisely.

If you stop communicating, you'll certainly grow apart. Not talking is like having a little bit of sand in your bed. You might not notice it at first, but then you begin feeling it more and more, until you can't stand it.

When we took our marriage vows, Robert and I promised that we would never go to bed without kissing each other. Okay, we've broken that vow a few times, but we do try to keep it.

My second cousin Tennessee Williams wrote a great line in *Cat on a Hot Tin Roof* when Big Mama points at a bed and says, "When a marriage goes on the rocks, the rocks are *there,* right *there!*" He sure got that one right!

A Love Lesson from Johnny Cash

Johnny and June were very spiritual, good people. I'll never forget the day that June wrapped her scenes for the movie

Thaddeus Rose and Eddie. It was on a Monday, but the rest of us still had many scenes to film, and this included Johnny.

"Well, I'll see you on Friday," June said after her last scene.

"You're done. What do you mean you'll see us on Friday?" I asked.

"Oh, I'm comin' back," she answered.

"All this way? Why don't you just relax at home?" I asked.

June Carter Cash just laughed, shook her head, and gave me some great marriage advice that made her a healer in her own right in a far different way. "Oh, Diane," she said, "Johnny and I have been married before. We've already had failed marriages, too. When we made our vows, we wrote out our rules. Honey, one of our rules is we aren't stupid."

I laughed, and June continued to confide the wisdom of the ages.

"No matter how much you love somebody, you don't leave each other alone for too long," she told me.

"Boy, you're smart," I said, with a nod of my head that conveyed my admiration for her logic.

By the way, she was back on Friday, bright and early, to visit her man. In the end, let me just say that June and Johnny were great people, and they were of the earth and accessible. They set a fine example of two individuals who went through hell along the way to find their great love.

MY LEFT FOOT

In 2004, I got a job offer to do Stephen King's *Kingdom Hospital*. It turned out to be an extremely tough shoot in Canada that got harder as we went along. Talk about negative energy—we shot in this abandoned warehouse in Vancouver two blocks away from a factory where they were burning carcinogenic body parts that had been removed from people during operations at the nearby hospital.

That poison air was blowing around. The warehouse set had an opening in the roof, and pigeons would fly in and roost above costumes. No wonder I ended up with mite bites.

Making matters worse, the weather was freezing cold, and the warehouse was on a river where the cold air whipped at us with such vengeance that we swore we might freeze in place. We walked on cement floors that were constantly being watered down so that they'd look "spooky." This just added to the damp gloom that was swirling around the actors.

My dressing room was right by the river, and the entire cast suffered constantly from the flu, colds, and fevers. Canadian doctors gave me the drug Cipro three times to get over the flu. I know they're not supposed to give this drug to children under 18 because it hurts their bones. Well, if it hurts children's bones, what does it do to you when you're over 40? I took the drug so that I could keep working, which was a big mistake.

Cold and lonely, I'd sit around one day doing nothing and then work 18 hours the next, which was exhausting. At 2 A.M., my knowledge of a diet goes right out the window and I say, "Give me that Snickers bar; give me that chocolate doughnut." I started putting on weight quickly, which was very hard on me because I'm usually in fighting shape.

An odd thing is happening with Canadian productions these days. Sadly, so many U.S. projects are filming in Canada to save money that there aren't enough trained crew members in the country to actually support all of the productions. The deal is that most of the crew actually waits until they're about two weeks from being done with a shoot and then quits in order to get the next plum job. That way they're never out of work, even for a day.

This happened on *Kingdom Hospital,* and the producers had to scramble and hire anyone they could find off the street to do the heavy lifting. These men were untrained and unfocused. One really didn't know what he was doing because he carried a huge, heavy light across the set while the actors were still present. Any experienced crew member knows that this should never happen because it's a recipe for someone getting seriously hurt and stopping the production, which costs an enormous amount of money.

One day toward the end of shooting, I was told to walk down a tiny staircase. At the same time, this particular man ran in my direction with the light and knocked me off the steps. Sharp pains shot through my ankle. I was immediately rushed to a Canadian hospital where they took an x-ray, but couldn't tell if the bone was cracked or not because it doesn't always show up right away after that type of injury.

Returning to the set on crutches, I was thrown into a scene that required the entire set to ignite with fire. "I'm not going to walk close to the fire on crutches," I said. "You're going to cut me out of that scene, because if anything goes wrong with the fire, I can't run!"

The untrained crew promised that nothing would go wrong. Guess what? We had sets painted with creosote, the same material that they use on telephone poles. When it's engulfed in flames, it turns carcinogenic; the walls of the set were also covered in this substance.

The crew lit the fire, and it didn't stay contained at all. Immediately, it burst out and started to spread across the set. Flames licked those carcinogenic walls, and the paint began to burn and produce thick, suffocating black smoke. The entire cast began to run for their lives, while I stood far away because at the last minute my wishes were honored—thank God—and I was cut out of the scene.

I truly believe that hurting my foot might have saved my life that day. I was told that my fellow actors Bruce Davison and Andrew McCarthy bolted for safety, literally running for their lives. Show business can be very hazardous to your health.

A few weeks later, I returned home on crutches. It was May, and my foot eventually healed.

That November should have been one of the happiest times in my life because my beautiful daughter Laura was scheduled to have her second baby at any moment. "Mom," she said in her sweet voice, "I want to have you close by when the time comes."

My immune system was a little shot after all of those months filming *Kingdom Hospital,* and unfortunately I got a nasty cold, which made me one miserable person. Springing into action, I called my doctor and asked for an antibiotic to get rid of any possible germs that would keep me away from my pregnant daughter.

My doctor's office called me back and said, "Diane, the doctor wants to prescribe a new drug for you. He thinks it will really knock out your cold quickly."

I'd never heard of this drug called Avelox, an antibiotic used for the management of common adult respiratory-tract infections. But trusting the doctor, I took one pill on Wednesday and I didn't feel good that night. I even told my husband, "I feel really strange."

Situations like this are when you must—must, must, must, must—trust your body and your instincts. But on Thursday morning, I popped another pill, and a few hours later stood up to get a glass of water. My ankle suddenly collapsed, and I fell to the floor screaming at the top of my lungs.

It was almost like a bomb going off in my body because I'd blown my tendon and re-cracked the metatarsal bone. Knowing that it was the prescription, I went to the doctor the following morning sobbing from the pain. Sure enough, he looked up the side effects of Avelox and found that one of the contraindications with this medication is that it can rupture tendons.

How many times do we take a drug and ignore all those horrifying side effects, thinking, *It will never happen to me*? Sweetie, you need to be vigilant about your own health and take warnings seriously. Of course, as a nation, we should also ask how the FDA sends drugs with horrifying side effects to an unsuspecting public.

I love those beautiful TV ads where a woman runs through a spring meadow saying that she feels as light as a butterfly after taking a little pill. Then there's the wake-up call in the form of an announcer who says: "This drug can cause heart attacks, strokes, blindness, and even death."

Hello, people! Why would you put something in your system that caused even *one* of those things—let alone all of them? It's actually disgusting to me. Don't we care about heart attacks, strokes, blindness, and even death? I could go on and on, but the point is that we need to really examine what and why the FDA is passing for the drug companies.

Eventually my tendon healed, but my passion for speaking out against pharmaceuticals and their little special surprises will never end. You see, even with all of my training, I was still in a hurry to take the new medication. I should have said to the doctor, "Okay, it's new. What are the side effects?"

One question can save your life. The first step to good health is using your brain.

MY MOTHER'S DEATH

My mother was aging nicely despite a few serious problems that had cropped up over the years. She'd had a little bone trouble and fallen and broken her hip, pelvis, and thigh. She healed each time, and at the age of 88, she was still doing yoga and stretching while walking every single day.

Her doctor put her on some pills, and she hid them from me. One of them was Vioxx, which the doctors told her would help with arthritis. In my opinion, it was this drug that caused my sweet mother to stroke out. She had one big stroke, and she regained consciousness in the hospital enough to talk to us, although she was very weak. By her bedside was a picture of the Virgin Mary.

One morning while Laura and I were keeping vigil, my mother looked toward the picture and said, "My God, would you please turn that light off."

"What light, Mother?" I asked.

"Diane, *this* light," she said in an exasperated voice, putting her hand on the picture of the Holy Mother. "Look at how bright it is! You've got to turn it off."

Laura and I looked at each other because we thought that the end was near. We ran into the other room sobbing to each other. "Oh my God, it's the end!" I gasped.

"She's dying—she's going!" Laura cried. "The Virgin Mary has come to lead the way."

From the other room, I heard my mother scream, "Diane! Laura!"

We ran back and asked her, "What is it mother?"

"Take this picture down," she insisted.

"I guess this means she's not ready to go. The little Leo wasn't even listening to the Virgin Mary," I told Laura. We prayed for a minute and then took the picture down.

She didn't go for a month. It took five more mini-strokes to send her back to God.

Now I have to tell you a little bit about the Lanier past. My parents loved each other, but there was a lot of Southern emotion there, which made it volatile at times. They even divorced when I was 17, even though my father never stopped loving my mother, and she never stopped caring for him. Both married other people.

Let's go back a minute. My father had a temper, although he was still an adorable, kind, smart man with a great sense of humor and wonderful charisma. Before my mother (Mary) married him, she was engaged to a fantastic man named Joe, and they were madly in love. Then along came my Daddy and swept Mary off her feet.

Joe was a gentle Catholic who never said a curse word, while my father was a cousin of Tennessee Williams and could cuss up a storm. He later cheated on my mother and broke her heart when she caught him. Years later after they were divorced, my father told me, "Diane, I never loved anyone the way I loved your mother. She had more class in her little finger than any woman I ever met in my life. She was so classy that I felt unworthy and not good enough for her. I wondered how she even loved me."

Women chased my father and he gave in. "It wasn't for sex," he told me. "I never had good sex like the kind I had with your mother because I loved her. I didn't cheat for love, but for ego. Men are damn fools, and my ego cost me the love of my life."

When my mother would get mad while they were still married, she'd tell my father, "I should have married my true love, Joe." Years later, after my parents were divorced and my mother remarried, she got a call from Joe's wife saying that he was in the hospital on his deathbed.

"It would mean the world to him to see you one last time before he died," said his wife. Talk about great devotion! She wanted her own husband to be happy for the last time by seeing his first love. My mother's husband, Dan, wanted her to go, but she was afraid to travel because she'd hurt her back and didn't want to get on a plane. My mother was scared and didn't go to Joe.

Then came Mary's time to die. As her daughter, I was sitting by her bedside one day and asked, "Mother, when you get to the other side and Daddy and Joe are there, who do you want to see first?"

"Joe—I want to see Joe!" said my angry mother. After all these years, she was still furious with my father.

A few days later, Laura and I were sitting with her. All of a sudden, my daughter turned to me and said, "Do you feel it? I feel Granddaddy in this room—I just feel it. He's come to escort her. He's here."

Later that day, I was reading stories to my mother and she stopped me midsentence. "Oh, Diane, honey, when I see your Daddy walking toward me, I'm going to be the happiest woman in the whole world," she said with a warm smile. For a minute I thought she was back in the past, still married to Daddy and just waiting for him to come home from work. I nodded as she continued to speak.

A slow smile spread across her face, and Mary said, "Honey, your Daddy's waiting for me. You know—up there."

My heart exploded with happiness and sadness. It was clear to me that although her first love would always have a place in her heart, my mother's true feeling was for my daddy. Why couldn't she have figured that out when he was still alive . . . and they were both healthy and young? Think of all the wasted time, lost moments, anger, and self-righteousness that keep us from hugging our loved ones just one more time.

For the first time in decades, the anger and the bullshit were gone. The manure that keeps us from seeing the sky had finally been cleaned up once and for all. . . . She died 24 hours later.

For a long time my mother didn't believe in past lives; she just wanted to go see Jesus. But in the last six months of her life, she talked of memories of other lifetimes. She had amazing growth during that period. She'd tell me, "There are a lot of things I still don't understand and much that I don't know; only God understands them."

Later on, they found out that Vioxx caused a lot of strokes, and unfortunately she'd been taking it— big time. The moral of the story is that you'd better really investigate the pills that you're taking. Don't let people make money on your ignorance. It's time to declare war when it comes to your health.

The Global Institute for Alternative Medicine tells us that "since the start of the Industrial Revolution, *thousands of new chemical agents* are used in food processing and preservation."

And here's the scariest fact of all from a Centers for Disease Control (CDC) scientist, Dr. James Pirkle: "If you gave a sample of blood or urine to us, we could find all sorts of things you didn't think you had. We are regularly, every day, exposed to 50,000 chemicals!"

Only a fraction of these chemicals have been studied for their effects on humans. There have been no studies at all showing the consequences of using these agents in varying combinations with each other. Living in such a toxic environment places our bodies under constant bombardment from every conceivable angle.

CHAPTER 18

RISING ABOVE DESPAIR

As president of the Art and Culture Task Force, a professional organization to promote culture in our country, I was in New York City to give a lecture about the health of the film industry—or should I say the virus called runaway productions that drive new movies and television shows to film in Canada, Europe, and Asia. I also spoke about culture in general and how we're harming the potential of future generations by cutting music, arts, and sports programs in schools. In my opinion, culture can be as powerful a weapon as a bomb. I made that statement on that crisp fall Monday evening in the Big Apple.

It had been a great trip that included seeing my friends Renée Taylor and Joe Bologna in their fabulous Broadway show *If You Ever Leave Me . . . I'm Going With You.* My close friend Lainie Kazan was doing *The Vagina Monologues,* and my dear Connie Stevens was singing in a New York club. All of us made a point of seeing each other and spending a little time catching up.

After my lecture, Robert and I moved out of our fancy lower Manhattan hotel and went over to my friend Avril Logan's house on the Upper East Side to spend a day with her before leaving the city. The next morning, the shrill jangling of the telephone woke us. My stepson Brandon demanded, "Quick—turn on the news! A plane just crashed into the World Trade Center!" It was September 11, 2001.

We ran upstairs to wake Avril, who was already at her window where you could see the clouds of death in the air. "I feel like I'm in the middle of a bad dream," she told us. I couldn't say a word and just stared at the black smoke on the horizon.

Lainie Kazan called a few minutes later screaming, "Where are you?! Are you safe? Have you heard the news?"

After calming her down, Robert told her, "We'll meet you for breakfast at that little coffee shop."

In silence, my husband and I walked through the city where I'd lived off and on for most of my life, where I'd been privileged to star on the Great White Way, and where my husband and I had fallen in love. For the first time since the Pilgrims, there were no cars or people. It was unbelievably quiet in the worst possible way. Eventually, we arrived at our old hangout, and even though it was packed, the place was deathly silent except for the occasional clank of a fork or spoon. Lainie was sitting at the counter. We moved toward each other and just started sobbing—we just kept hugging her until our sobs became tiny little cries.

A few minutes later, my cell phone was ringing. It was Connie Stevens's daughter Joely Fisher yelling, "Diane, I can't get my mother! Do you think something happened to her? You have to find out!"

We had to go clear across town to West 60th Street to find out about Connie, and frankly I was frantic, too. Her condo wasn't that far from the World Trade Center, and we began what turned out to be a long walk to find our friend. Once in a while, a cab sped past with the words "off duty" flashing. No one was taking any fares.

It seemed impossible, but one lone taxi finally stopped in front of us. "I'm not supposed to do it, lady, but I'll take you to Central Park for 30 bucks," said the cabbie in a thick accent.

Robert handed him the money, and we piled in. On a regular day, the ride to the park would be about five to seven dollars, tops.

"How long have you been in this country?" Robert asked the cabbie.

"Six years," he replied. "I've been a citizen for one."

"And you'd charge a fellow American citizen five times what this ride is worth on a day like today?" Then Robert pulled out his wallet again and said, "You must need money desperately, so here's another ten. Go buy your wife a drink."

Silently, our fellow American dropped us off at the east park entrance. By the way, he took the extra ten bucks and stuffed it in his pocket without so much as a "Thank you."

We walked the miles through Central Park to get to the west side. The type of quiet that surrounded us had never been heard before in the city—and thankfully hasn't existed since. All I could hear was the rustle of fall leaves. This was interrupted by the occasional F15 streaking across the sky, one of the few sounds that New Yorkers didn't usually hear in the streets.

We found our friend safe, but in shock. Renée Taylor Bologna, who was in New Jersey that morning, had called Connie at what felt like the crack of dawn with the chilling news. "Connie, quick, get up!" Renée insisted. "A plane has crashed into the World Trade Center."

Connie vaulted out of bed, turned on the TV, and then gazed through her picture window with its direct view of the towers, one of which was now ominously belching black smoke into the clear morning air. She stared at what she and all of New York still thought was a monstrous accident, and then she was startled by the sound of an aircraft through her west window. It was at eye level flying in over the Hudson River.

Planes never fly in over the river. What in God's name is it doing? Connie wondered as she followed the plane with her eyes . . . as it turned toward the second tower and then flew right into it. In total shock, she spent the next several minutes watching the people jump out of the flaming buildings.

As we all know, this was one of the greatest tragedies ever perpetrated on the American people. I immediately wondered if we could ever heal from the wound. On that day, I couldn't envision a future without fear, and at first I saw America spiraling down as a country.

How could this have been allowed to happen? Unanswered questions haunted me. However, in the following days I saw my country bucking up like never before—I saw what makes America great.

Of course, during that period my son-in-law, Ben Harper, had everyone trying to find us. He and Laura were frantic because they hadn't received the message that we were at Avril's house. We finally got in touch with them, and Robert reserved a Lincoln Town Car to drive home—and cancelled it when we heard that the planes would soon be flying again. But then we discovered that air travel really had been stopped, and by that time all the rental cars were gone. I remember not knowing what to do, so Robert and I just took to the streets and walked down Broadway.

We became part of an impromptu gathering on the pavement. All the restaurants were passing out candles, and people had come out of their homes and lined up on both sides of the streets. We were hugging and praying. In the midst of such utter devastation, there was this quiet coming together that brought tears to my eyes and soothed my broken heart. I was wrong about that downward spiral; even in great tragedy there's an evolution that makes your heart soar. I'm certain of one thing: There are a lot of sides to the word *truth*. All of us need to explore all the angles in order to keep our country free.

By the way, Robert and I finally rented the largest available car on Saturday, a Chevy Lumina, and made our way all 3,000 miles back to Los Angeles with Connie Stevens in the backseat. I'm sure those days transformed us forever, as they did everybody. I believe that *everything* alters everyone; insanity is when nobody changes. This is what spiraling is all about, folks!

I was astounded by the bravery that I saw on September 11. Anyone who helps a human being try to find his or her loved ones humbles me. I witnessed good deeds and acts of caring among my fellow human beings that restored my own faith in humanity.

You never know who will rise to the task when things happen. Have you ever seen braver men and women than those who serve in the fire and police departments? I came to realize during those days that courage is an amazing quality. It's like sainthood, in that it's a true act of love in caring for your fellow humans. It makes me cry just to think about it, but I hate that it takes acts of horror to make us remember how important we are to each other as a human family.

I knew in those moments that I'd write about this someday in a series of what I call "philosophy letters" for my grandchildren. The first question I'd try to answer for them is simple: *What have we done to make people hate us so much? What am*

I not being told that we've done that makes the world feel this way about us? What's really going on?

In 1984, I went with ten women on a fact-finding tour to El Salvador, Honduras, and Nicaragua. I must tell you—and I'm being completely honest here—that we were Catholic, Jewish, Methodist, Baptist, Jehovah's Witness, Lutheran, and Episcopalian. We represented whites, blacks, Asians, Indians, and other folk—the full spectrum. We were completely different women from vastly dissimilar walks of life. But when we returned to the United States, we had one thing in common that bonded us: We were angry with our government. George Orwell's *1984* had come true right on time.

Governments are like people—they're not perfect. I think of it from the perspective of a mother: If you have five kids and one of them is doing something bad, then you gotta find out about it and do something to help change the situation for the better and alleviate the negatives. It follows that if your Congressional representative isn't doing right, remember that that person is your voice. You're paying his or her salary, and you have to do something about it as this person's employer.

I also believe that the bigger they are, the harder they fall, whether it's your president or your cleaning lady. Each person on this earth needs integrity. We can all slip, and certainly we can all make a mistake and say I'm sorry. But it's not all right to lie like a dirty, rotten dog about what's going on in the world. It's not okay to do something bad to another country and then pretend that they're doing something bad to us.

Our reputation as Americans isn't so good all over the world right now, and we need to know exactly why. We can say that people are irrational and crazy everywhere else. Hey, all of us can be a little nutty at times, and that includes yours truly. But what has America done to make everybody hate us so much? It's a question in the back of all of our minds these days, but one I can't seem to get answered.

Why are we "the American devil" to the world? I look around my own country and think, *Most of the people I see are wonderful. We have great people who make up this nation.* Sure, we have some nasty folk, with a few mean ones who have to be stopped, but by and large, I love the people in this country.

I believe that the first step in fixing the world situation is to get rid of those people lying to us. They're a cancer, and they have to be removed. But how do you start? It's rather easy, in that you just ask questions. It's not the answers in life that are important; it's what you ask. If you want to take my grandson into battle, you better damn well have some answers, because I'm asking some questions.

I spent a lot of my time on that trip with women's rights leader Bella Abzug. She told me stories that were so upsetting, including one about how she was booked on *Nightline,* but was told the day of the taping that she wasn't wanted anymore on the show. She heard that government officials had called to complain about her speaking out, so she was informed that she wouldn't be appearing that night. In a land of democracy, that's not right, folks.

The women from my overseas trip gave as many interviews as possible when we returned. Many major-media outlets came and taped the interviews, eager to learn what was going on in the world, yet the only network that aired our views was CBS because I was starring in the *Alice* TV series at the time on that network. Where were the other stations?

CHAPTER 19

SPIRALING INTO THE FUTURE

The other day I was stopped at a red light when I saw a man and his dog in the crosswalk in front of me, with a second dog tagging along behind. Just as the light changed, the car next to me was revving its engine. Sticking my head out of the window of my car, I shouted a warning: "Sir, your dog behind you is going to get hit!"

Glancing back, he replied, "Oh, it's not mine." He continued to walk, ignoring the poor creature that was now a target for passing cars.

Angry with the man and panicked for the animal, I momentarily blocked the traffic with my car, jumped out, and quickly retrieved the little lost dog. He was wearing a collar complete with an ID tag, so I immediately contacted his owners, who only lived three blocks away. The distraught elderly couple was so ecstatic to see their darling Mikey. With tears in their eyes, they thanked me profusely for saving his life.

Again, I felt anger when I thought about the man in the crosswalk. His words "It's not mine" echoed through my head. That dog could have been killed, its essence snuffed out, and the old couple's life horribly affected and irrevocably changed. It took me only minutes of my time to help a dog and two human beings. That's what we're here for: to serve the Creative God Force within each other and ourselves. It's as simple as that.

"It's not mine!" he said.

Mine? My child is yours, and your child is mine. We must put our children on our shoulders so that perhaps they'll see further than we have. Then maybe this world of ours will become humane and whole.

A doctor once told me something that helps me each and every single time I began to spiral out of control. He said, "Diane, you'll be battered around because you lead with your heart and not your head. But before this life is over, you'll be a big winner because you'll be true to yourself." I wish more people led with their hearts; I think it would be a better world.

In the '80s, everything about this life began to open for me and everyone else, as the universe went through what's known as a "paradigm shift" The good news is we're beginning other such movements; we're starting to delve into cosmic consciousness.

By now you're probably wondering, *What does this all mean, Diane?* To put it simply, we're all starting to realize that in some strange way, we're all part of each other. I'm you, you're me, and we are. If your little finger gets injured, your toe may not know it—but might pay the price. Humanity is one body. When part of that being is hurting, the rest of us may not pay attention, but we may pay for it.

I do thank God that we live in a country where we can express our views. We don't have to be afraid to speak our minds. Just don't make your point the wrong way. Speak, and then stop and listen for the next opinion—you might just learn something.

I still see hatred in this world, and when it gets to be too much, I remind myself that God is the Creator and has more than one child. I tell myself that the Almighty loves us all. The pattern of life is a square dance, and it always comes around. God help the country that's hurting another. Lord have mercy on the United Nations and those leaders who profiteer and aren't standing up and fulfilling their great opportunities of leadership with every ounce of their being.

If we're going to evolve into the Aquarian Age, we have to work a little bit harder, clean up our acts, and be accountable. But it will be worth it. I promise you.

In order to have a healthy physical body, we have to create *balance*. And to have a country that's whole and well, we have to do the same thing. The right equilibrium is also necessary for a healthy planet—and it starts with the individual.

Sweet God, help us. There have been so many wars in the history of our little planet, so many lives lost, and for what? Everyone on both sides of the fence thinks that they're right, and the enemy sits on the other side, so they must be wrong . . . right?

There's been so much bloodshed. If we can't even get along with our own neighbors in our own country, how on earth do we think that we can get along with other nations? The answer is communication, as it's the only "weapon" that can bring understanding.

We have a Department of Defense that deals in war toys to defend us from the evils of the world, which we clearly need. But I haven't heard a better idea than that proposed by Congressman Dennis Kucinich's legislation for a Peace Alliance. By any other name, it's still the idea of our lifetime. Along with others, my friend and author Marianne Williamson has created a citizens' campaign to help support this legislation for a Department of Peace.

Okay, I think there's time for one last story. After all, I do come from Mississippi, and we Southerners are story-tellers—it's our birthright.

A few years back I was about to speak to 1,200 people at the American Holistic Medical Association in Phoenix, Arizona. The night before my lecture, I was finishing a shoot in Los Angeles and had a long, challenging day with Gavin MacLeod on his series *The Love Boat.* That evening we were both obligated to attend an ABC-TV network-affiliates dinner.

As we were eating chocolate mousse, Gavin leaned over to me and asked, "Diane, what's the matter? You seem upset."

"Well, I've goofed," I said. "I'm being picked up at 4:30 in the morning to catch a plane for Arizona to give a lecture. I try to tailor each talk I give depending on the energy I feel on that day, but I haven't had any time to go over my notes, meditate, or prepare for tomorrow, and it's already midnight. How did I allow this to happen? I'm feeling so vulnerable."

At that moment, our waiter interrupted me. As he poured the wine, he whispered, "Excuse me, Miss Ladd. I'm a great fan of your acting, but I want to share something else with you. I attended your lecture a couple of months ago in L.A. at the Whole Life Expo. . . ." His chin quivered slightly as he continued: "I've just been through a devastating experience. My partner has HIV, and I've been feeling helpless and very angry."

With tears welling in his eyes he said, "Well, you made me understand when you said, 'We're not God, just a part of God, and that part of us is in Earth's school and learning. We're in God's school.'"

At that moment, a very impatient man from the next table yelled, "Waiter! Bring us another bottle of mineral water!"

The server brushed aside his tears, smiled, and started to walk away to get the water. Then he came back over to me and said, "Xeroxed your brochure and gave 'em to all my friends. I just wanted to thank you. Maybe someday you can write a book for all of us, too."

Before I could even speak, he hurried off, and then a gentle pat on my shoulder turned me toward Gavin's smiling face. "That's your affirmation and your lecture for tomorrow, kiddo!" he exclaimed with a grin.

I didn't feel quite so vulnerable anymore. At that moment, I realized once again that there are windows of grace. Life is still about connections and points where our destinies begin each day anew.

Thomas Merton said, "Silence is the primary language of God." How odd that in this faster-paced society of our present modern-day mechanized world, we have so little time to enjoy the golden treasure of silence. Perhaps that's why more and more of us are participating in meditation, and more and more spiritual groups are arranging gatherings of like minds who feel the need for peace, harmony, and kindness. Having been raised in Catholicism, a current student of Kabbalah, and at present also an ordained minister, I go where the good is . . . for example, on Sunday evenings in Austin, Texas, the First Baptist Church on Trinity has an exquisitely beautiful, peaceful, and inspiring service. There are many of these now taking place with different groups throughout the country; you just have to find them.

I'd like to leave you with the following: God gave us two eyes to see, two ears to hear, and one mouth with which to speak. So the final lesson is to look and listen twice, but only speak once. Hear your fellow human beings with both ears, but more important, listen with the ear of your heart.

That doesn't mean that you can't kick up your heels a little bit in this life and fight for all that's good, righteous, and honorable. Remember my motto: *Have a little faith, kick a little dirt.*

🌪 🌪 🌪

ACKNOWLEDGMENTS

My thanks to:

Dr. Gladys McGarey, the first woman president of the American Holistic Medical Association (AHMA)—AMA doctors who not only practice current medicine but believe in the merits of alternative modalities.

Dr. Terry Friedman, dedicated physician/author/lecturer, internist on the American Board of Family Practice, and one of the founders of the AHMA. ("In order to find a cure, you must find the cause.")

Congressman Berkley Bedell of Iowa, having been told he only had three months to live from Lyme disease, was cured thanks to the suggestion of a veterinarian friend to consume colustrum from a pregnant cow. Bedell, with his own money, founded the National Foundation for Alternative Medicine in Washington, D.C.

Daniel Haley, the New York legislator, and the author of *Politics in Healing.*

Steve Anderson, R.N., B.S.N., certified holistic nurse, and renowned instructor for Healing Touch International.

Dr. Doug Nelson, a sensitive and caring physician who enabled my mother, Mary, to make a diginified transition.

Dr. Cynthia Watson, Santa Monica, California, who fulfills the Hippocratic Oath.

Dr. Green, endocrinologist, Thousand Oaks, California, a genius who really knows and cares about his patients and his work.

Dr. Viola Frymann, founder of the Osteopathic Promise for Children, San Diego, California, another genius who has raised the level of medicine to a higher level.

Congressman Dan Burton of Indiana, a fighter for truth and fair play in the medical arena.

Congresswoman Karen McCarthy of Missouri, a teacher fighting for the people and the country.

Dr. Ted L. Edwards, Jr., Austin, Texas, Olympic medical consultant.

Mentors, deceased:

Dr. Jules Bernhardt, leader in the power of mind research.

C.C. Bateman, war hero from Pappy Boyington's Black Sheep Squadron, my teacher, and one of the top dream analyzers and aura readers in our country; protégé of the late, great Edgar Cayce.

Sri Swami Satchidananda, a leader in spiritual teachings. Chosen from the world's religious leaders to bless the first meeting of the United Nations in the new millennium.

Teacher and friend Lee Strasberg, one of the founders of the famed Actors Studio, the largest and most prestigious acting/directing/playwright group in the world.

Shelley Winters, actress/writer (a national treasure!) and my daughter's godmother.

Jocelyn Brando, one of the greatest comedy actresses that ever blessed the American stage, adopted sister and friend who kept me on the mark.

Norman Garey, brother by marriage, attorney, inspiring advisor and friend.

Sister Mary Gertrude, Mississippi high-school teacher. ("Diane, perseverance is what counts.")

Marlon Brando, the "king of actors" and my greatest acting inspiration, who allowed me to argue with him. He was a good friend who wrote to me just before he died: "Diane, if I had your perseverance, my whole life might have been different!"

Mary Bernadette Ladnier Garey, my mother, who taught me gentleness, tenderness, and caring.

Preston Paul Ladnier, my daddy, a veterinarian of sorts, and developer of a line of poultry and animal medicines; songwriter and singer; student of humanity. ("Diane, you can do any by-God thing you make up your mind to do in this world!")

Friends and family:

Glenda Christian and Bill Young, teachers of meditation and ageless spiritual wisdom.

Friend and editor Gael Belden.

My editors, Jill Kramer (at Hay House) and Cindy Pearlman.

Assistants Rita Claggett and Bonnie White, who kicked dirt so I could focus on the book.

My sheltie dog, Journey, whose affection keeps me smiling on my journey.

My cat, Sunshine, who teaches me affection and independence.

My grandchildren, who make me realize that if I win all the Oscars in the world but leave the planet as a sewer for them to roll around in, I haven't accomplished much.

My daughter, Laura Dern, without whom this book would never have taken place.

My husband, Robert Charles Hunter, whose patience and love is a mantle of light inspiring my life.

And my special thanks to all who so kindly and graciously endorsed this book.

ABOUT THE AUTHOR

Diane Ladd is internationally acclaimed as a three-time Oscar nominee, three-time Emmy nominee, and the recipient of 23 awards, which include the British Academy Award, the Independent Spirit Award, and a Golden Globe. She's been heralded by *Time* magazine as "one of the ten top actresses, not only in this country, but in the whole world." Diane and her daughter, Laura Dern, made show-business history as the only mother/daughter in tandem to be nominated for an Oscar in the same film *(Rambling Rose)*.

Diane is an actress, writer, director, nutritional consultant, lecturer, healer, and ordained minister. She can entertain you; and if something makes you sick, she can heal you. And if that doesn't work, she can bury you! She's a very good friend to have.

Diane is a member of the Board of Advisors for the National Foundation of Alternative Medicine, having worked with many notable doctors for more than 20 years. She's a lifetime member of the famed Actors Studios actors, directors, and playwrights unit; and she's a National Board member of the Screen Actors Guild. In 2005, she co-starred in the film *The World's Fastest Indian* with Anthony Hopkins, and co-starred with Ashley Judd in the Sundance Festival's opening selection, *Come Early Morning*. She's also filming *Woman Inside,* the true story of the late Martha Mitchell. Most recently, Diane was awarded the Susan B. Anthony's "Failure is Impossible" achievement award.

Website: **www.dianeladd.com**

We hope you enjoyed this Hay House book. If you'd like to receive a free catalog featuring additional Hay House books and products, or if you'd like information about the Hay Foundation, please contact:

Hay House, Inc.
P.O. Box 5100
Carlsbad, CA 92018-5100

(760) 431-7695 or **(800) 654-5126**
(760) 431-6948 (fax) or **(800) 650-5115 (fax)**
www.hayhouse.com® • **www.hayfoundation.org**

Published and distributed in Australia by: Hay House Australia Pty. Ltd. • 18/36 Ralph St. • Alexandria NSW 2015 • *Phone:* 612-9669-4299 • *Fax:* 612-9669-4144 • www.hayhouse.com.au

Published and distributed in the United Kingdom by: Hay House UK, Ltd. • Unit 62, Canalot Studios • 222 Kensal Rd., London W10 5BN • *Phone:* 44-20-8962-1230 • *Fax:* 44-20-8962-1239 • www.hayhouse.co.uk

Published and distributed in the Republic of South Africa by: Hay House SA (Pty), Ltd., P.O. Box 990, Witkoppen 2068 • *Phone/Fax:* 27-11-706-6612 • orders@psdprom.co.za

Published in India by: Hay House Publications (India) Pvt. Ltd., 3 Hampton Court, A-Wing, 123 Wodehouse Rd., Colaba, Mumbai 400005 • *Phone:* 91 (22) 22150557 or 22180533 • *Fax:* 91 (22) 22839619 • www.hayhouseindia.co.in

Distributed in India by: Media Star, 7 Vaswani Mansion, 120 Dinshaw Vachha Rd., Churchgate, Mumbai 400020 • *Phone:* 91 (22) 22815538-39-40 • *Fax:* 91 (22) 22839619 • booksdivision@mediastar.co.in

Distributed in Canada by: Raincoast • 9050 Shaughnessy St., Vancouver, B.C. V6P 6E5 • *Phone:* (604) 323-7100 • *Fax:* (604) 323-2600

Tune in to **HayHouseRadio.com**™ for the best in inspirational talk radio featuring top Hay House authors! And, sign up via the Hay House USA Website to receive the Hay House online newsletter and stay informed about what's going on with your favorite authors. You'll receive bimonthly announcements about: Discounts and Offers, Special Events, Product Highlights, Free Excerpts, Giveaways, and more!
www.hayhouse.com®